GROWING UP CATHOLIC,

IN PHILLY, DURING THE 50s AND 60s WITH A VERY CONTROLLING MOTHER

GROWING UP CATHOLIC,

IN PHILLY, DURING THE 50s AND 60s WITH A VERY CONTROLLING MOTHER

Richard Etherton

PALMETTO
PUBLISHING
Charleston, SC
www.PalmettoPublishing.com

Copyright © 2024 by Richard Etherton

All rights reserved

No portion of this book may be reproduced, stored in a retrieval system, or transmitted in any form by any means—electronic, mechanical, photocopy, recording, or other—except for brief quotations in printed reviews, without prior permission of the author.

Hardcover ISBN: 979-8-8229-5399-4
Paperback ISBN: 979-8-8229-5400-7
eBook ISBN: 979-8-8229-5401-4

Dedication

I dedicate this book to my wonderful wife, Connie. She has been my inspiration in writing my life story. Connie is, and has been, the confident, guiding light in my life and the mother of two beautiful children. She has been with me since we were 16, through good times and dark times. Connie has always helped me to see the better road to follow, and to handle adversity. I believe the secret to our success is mutual respect and, above all, love, even when it is tested. I pray to God to continue our fantastic relationship for many years to come.
I will always love you Connie!

Contents

Preface ix
September 1955: First Grade, Age 6, at Holy Child Parish School 1
September 1956: Second Grade, Age 7 5
September 1957: Third Grade, Age 8. 8
September 1958: Fourth Grade, Age 9. 17
September 1959: Fifth Grade, Age 10 30
September 1960: Sixth Grade, Age 11 36
September 1961: Seventh Grade, Age Twelve 41
September 1962: Eighth Grade, Age Thirteen 44
Photo Album 49
September 1963: Age Fourteen, Freshman Year of High School
at Cardinal Dougherty 61
September 1964: Second Year at High School, Age Fifteen 66
September 1965: Third Year at High School, Age Sixteen. 71
September 1966: Fourth Year at High School, Age Seventeen 72
Other Stuff and Sayings. 83
Atlantic City. 86
Clothes, Christmas, the Infamous Haircut, and Other Stuff 91
Conclusions 99

Preface

I was born in Philadelphia on 16 February 1949 at the Philadelphia Naval Hospital. I am an only child–no siblings.

My mother's maiden name was Irene C. DeMark (the old-world name was DeMarko, changed to DeMark when her father immigrated to the United States prior to 1900).

She was born and lived with her five siblings (three male two female) on the 2100 block of Earp Street in South Philadelphia. My mother attended West Catholic High School for Girls and was the only one in her family to graduate with a high school diploma. She experienced the hard times of the Great Depression, and on a daily basis, reminded me of her sacrifices during those years. My mother didn't work outside the house while I was in grade school.

My father's name was Dewey Etherton, born in 1899 in Red Cloud, Nebraska, growing up in Bowling Green, Kentucky. My dad rarely spoke of his early years before he joined the U.S. Navy in 1919. My father served on submarines during WWII and saw action in all major battles in the Pacific. He retired from the Navy in 1949 as a Chief Petty Officer E-7 grade, MMC, with thirty years of service. He received several meritorious awards during the war years. Since my father was serving in the Navy, he did not experience any of the depression-related life. After his retirement from the Navy, he worked as a supervisor for the Philadelphia Water Department. He retired from this job in 1970.

We were classified as a middle-income family.

We resided at 4817 North 15th Street, in a section of North Philadelphia identified as Logan. These houses were of the typical inner-city style of row homes built adjacent to each other. Your walls were part of your neighbors' walls on each side of your house. Except our house was only one of two on our street which had a driveway and a detached garage. This type of house was described by the realtors as "semi-detached."

Being of the Catholic religion, our parish was the Church of the Holy Child on the 5200 block of Broad Street. This parish had a beautiful main church constructed of stone and in the Gothic style, with a center dome that was visible for miles. Directly adjacent to the main church building was the original church, now designated as the chapel. The chapel had a very large basement area, which was used for social events, school dances, and scout meetings. In the late 50s, due to the "baby boom," the basement was divided into four classrooms. There were three floors built on top of the Chapel, which was the parish school. Grades first through eighth were taught at the Holy Child Parish School.

The church also owned two residential row houses on Carlisle Street, which directly formed the west side of the church property. These two houses were located near the intersection of West Fishers Avenue to the north. The two houses were of a two-story type of construction, with basements, and the main floor and the second floor were completely gutted to form open-type classrooms. This location was identified as the "School Annex Buildings." There was a single-use bathroom facility on each floor, a precursor to today's "unisex" bathrooms. Due to the overcrowding at the main school building, second-grade students received their education at the School Annex Buildings.

I remember my mother sitting with me and reading to me from the Little Golden Books. I did enjoy listening to the stories. My earliest memories prior to preschool are of my grandmother in South Philly. My mother and father would drive from our house on 15th Street to my grandmother's house on Earp Street. Her house was of the typical two-story Philly row house, brick construction. We would enter into the kitchen, which had a long table in the center of the room.

My grandmother, her sister Kate, my mother and father, and my aunt Betty would be there all seated. There was no TV to watch, and my mother didn't bring any of my toys for me to play with. I was told to "sit at the table and be still, stop moving around." Everyone at the table would be smoking their ciggies except my father and Aunt Betty. I remember my father saying that he was going to Mulligans Bar to get pitchers of beer. My grandmother went to a kitchen cabinet and got two glass pitchers. She then went to the refrigerator and took out the butter dish and proceeded to wipe butter all on the insides of the two glass pitchers. My father took the pitchers and me, and we walked up to 22nd Street, a short distance to Mulligans Bar.

I remember this place vividly. There was a huge neon sign hanging outside the place in the form of a boxing glove. I went into the bar with my father; this place seemed very strange to me. The place had a foul smell of beer and cigarettes. There were a lot of men standing around the bar, talking, smoking, and laughing. There were these large brass pots around the front of the bar. I asked my father what these were for, and he said they were "spittoons," and the men would spit in them. There were pictures on the walls of boxers with writing below them. My dad gave the two pitchers to the man behind the bar and asked him to fill the pitchers. We left the bar with the two pitchers full of beer and walked back to my grandmother's house. On the way back, I asked my dad why butter was rubbed in the pitchers; Grandmom said it gave the beer a better taste.

We walked back to my grandmother's house and put the two pitchers of beer on the kitchen table. Everyone started drinking the beer and smoking their ciggies. There was nothing for me to drink, no milk, soda, or juice; I had water and was told by my mother to "sit still and be quiet." Eventually we left and drove back to 15th Street. Every time we visited my grandmother in South Philly, my father and I would take the two "buttered beer pitchers" and walk to Mulligans Bar.

Prior to attending the first grade at the Holy Child Parish School, my mother enrolled me for the 1954 fall session in preschool at the Saint Mary's Academy located at Somerville Avenue on Old York Road. This facility was approximately a quarter mile north of the Holy Child Parish. The "school day" was a half-day session from morning to noon five days a week. My mother arranged for livery service to and from Saint Mary's. The transportation consisted of being picked up at the house in a Plymouth station wagon, driven to Saint Mary's and then picked up at noon and driven home. There were approximately five to six school-age kids in this car being dropped off at various school locations. This occurred in 1955, well before the age of seat belts in cars–none of us in the car were strapped in. I can vividly remember my mother handing me two quarters (fifty cents) on Monday mornings to hand to the driver of the station wagon. The fifty cents was the payment for the entire week of pickup and drop-off. I can also remember the lady driver's name, Mrs. Hamaslager.

The school day at Saint Mary's consisted of being taught the basic Catholic prayers, standing straight at your desk when praying, correctly folding your hands in prayer, gazing skyward when praying, pledging allegiance to the flag, sitting upward in your chair and folding your hands at your desk, talking only when allowed to speak, learning how to count to ten and learning the alphabet, and starting to write your name in cursive. And this was all driven by the Saint Joseph nuns. This was also my first exposure to forming up in straight lines and walking/moving in a group. This was always accompanied by the nuns barking out "no talking," and "put the sign of the cross on your lips."

Saint Mary's Academy was a private Catholic school offering classes from preschool to eighth grade. The only remarkable event that I can remember is that there was a Christmas play at Saint Mary's. All of the grades performed some type of act: singing, dancing, or reciting a poem. The preschool group performed some type of skit; I really can't remember the specifics. I do remember that we wore our pajamas on stage, and we wore bright red lipstick.

Our parents and friends were invited to be in the audience. I remember seeing flash bulbs going off as pictures were taken. Of course my mother did not take any pictures, as she only had a Kodak Brownie camera without a flash attachment! For your information, she never purchased a flash attachment, could not take pictures inside, and only took black and white photos. She always said, "I don't like color pictures." The show ended with someone stepping on the bottom of my pajamas and ripping the lower half of the leg. The experience at Saint Mary's ended without any fanfare or earth-shattering revelations. I remember my mother getting bent out of shape, trying to find who stepped on my pajamas and ripped them.

The time between the end at Saint Mary's and the start of first grade at Holy Child was spent being hounded by my mother on the "proper way to behave in school." I remember that a portion of every day was dedicated to sitting straight in a chair at the kitchen table, folding my hands on the table, reciting my prayers, and practicing my handwriting and numbers. My mother drummed into my head, "Don't ever called them nuns, they are to be referred to as sisters."

I will now describe, in as much detail as I can remember, my formative years of Catholic education at the Holy Child Parish School. Seven of my eight years of schooling were administered by the Sisters of the Saint Joseph Order. These gems had absolutely NO concept of how a normal family functioned. I am convinced these nuns had no feelings or respect for adolescent children. I think they viewed the children as some type of demon, and it was their God-given duty to beat them into submission. I know they fostered deep hatred for the male students, as they actually reveled in a hidden joy when slapping, punching, and shaking one of the boys. Many comments were made that the nuns were frustrated old bags placed there to punish the students during the school day.

September 1955

First Grade, Age 6, at Holy Child Parish School

My mother made arrangements with one of the girls across the street from our house. She would give the girl fifty cents a week to walk me to school in the mornings, back home at lunchtime, back to school after lunch, and finally home at the end of the school day. We lived only four city blocks from our house to the school, but Mom was concerned about my safety? Halfway through the school year, my mother arranged for Mrs Hamaslager to drive me to school and home at the end of the day. Arriving at school on the first day, we all stood around talking to each other in the school yard. I was looking for my friends from the neighborhood. I was amazed at the number of children gathered in one place. The number of nuns standing around was unbelievable to a small child like me. It looked like a convention of penguins!

One of the nuns began to ring a handheld bell, a schoolyard bell. The nuns began to walk around the group, hollering, "Get in line, children, and no talking, make the sign of the cross on your lips." WOW, what an initiation to the first day of school. Each nun would break off into a separate group, hollering out, "Grade one over here, second grade over here," and so on through all eight grades. Then the nuns would gather their assembled group of children and literally march them up to the floor where the assigned school rooms were. This was my first exposure to the nuns' favorite item of intimidation, the clicker, or as some called it, the cricket. This metallic object, when held between the thumb and index finger and squeezed, made a fairly loud chirping sound. You would hear this annoying sound all day long when inside the school building. A nun was never without her clicker.

The constant verbal order of "no talking" was belted out as we made it the classrooms. The first-grade classrooms were on the first floor of the school building. We stood in the hallway as one of the three nuns called out our names and assigned us to a classroom. There were three first-grade classrooms. When we all had entered the classroom, the nuns assigned seating in an alphabetical order. When the clouds settled, we all rose to our feet and recited our morning prayers, then the pledge of allegiance to the flag. There were one hundred children in the room that I was assigned to. Some of the children in the room began to cry uncontrollably, calling for their mothers. The nun would come down to the child and tell them to stop crying, as it was not going to be accepted in her classroom. The nun did not show any compassion or understanding to the child. I told my mother what happened, and she said that the sisters knew what they were doing. Really, Mom?

The learning experience consisted of exposure to more prayers, catechism instruction, memorizing the Ten Commandments, preparing for your first holy communion, basic math, spelling, reading, and health habits instructions. The nun in my classroom would always call on the same child to answer a question, go to the blackboard, and participate in classroom activities. I was never called for anything. There were scheduled bathroom breaks during the day. The boys' bathroom dates back to when the building was constructed. They were the long-style urinals placed against the outer wall. The boys and girls were marched to the "lavatories" in single file lines, being told, "No talking, make the sign of the cross on your lips." The boys were led to the boys' room by the nun, who allowed only three or four boys in the room at one time. The nun would blurt out, "Do your business quickly, no talking or looking around." There were occasions when the nun would actually walk into the lavatory when the little boys were taking a leak. I guess that the nun wanted to take a peek at some of the little peckers as they were taking a piss. Just frustrated old bitties. I told my mom about this, and she just looked at me and made a remark that nuns don't do things like that. Really, Mom, I witnessed it! There was always some child getting sick in the classroom, throwing up all over the place. Some children were so sick they were sent to the nurse's office and their parent had to come and take them home.

Christmas in first grade was eye-opening. We rehearsed singing Christmas carols for an upcoming visit from Santa on the last day before Christmas break. On that last day, all of the grades were assembled in the chapel and each grade sang the carols to an audience comprised of the priests from the parish. Santa appeared (he was one of the older students), and gift-wrapped boxes of candy were handed out to each student. The candy was furnished by a local candymaker called Dairy Maid, with their store on the 5100 block of Broad Street. I took my box of candy home, and when I entered the front door, my mother, upon seeing the box of candy, immediately took it from me. She examined the twelve pieces of chocolate and began to squeeze them. The filling began to ooze out of each piece of candy. My mother then began to select pieces of candy to eat. She asked if I wanted any of the candy–I said no. Who wants any candy that has been destroyed, even if by your mother.

First grade was somewhat uneventful, without any major issues. We were introduced to going to church on the first Fridays of the month, that attendance at mass on Sundays was absolutely required; if you were sick and could not attend, a note from your parents was required when you came to school on Monday. You were given donation envelopes on Fridays before you left school. The nun instructed you to write your name on the envelope and classroom number and place your contribution in the envelope with your name and classroom number on the outside of the envelope. It was later discovered that the nuns reviewed the envelopes, and that was how they determined who was at church on Sunday.

I experienced my first Easter Sunday in church. My Easter Sunday garb consisted of a collage of mismatched pants and a sport coat that was at least two sizes too small. My mother was not one to buy me a suit because it would require alterations to the trousers– which at the time was probably a whole three dollars. We were being prepared and receiving instructions for making our first Holy Communion, which occurred in May. My mother was livid since she had to purchase a white suit, white shirt, and white shoes for me to participate in this religious event. I remember going to a local men's and boy's clothing store, Robert Hall. My mother instructed the salesman that she wanted an inexpensive white suit, large enough so I wear it both this year for the Communion and next year for my Confirmation. She paid for alterations, but just enough for the white suit to fit me like a tent. The white shirt was also oversized to wear next year. Even at this young age, I felt like an ass hole sloshing around in this oversized garb.

First grade ended with me getting good marks and being promoted to second grade.

September 1956

Second Grade, Age 7

The new school year began in the same fashion as the previous year, meeting outside and looking around for the friendly faces that you knew from last year. I told my mother that there were fewer kids in school this year. She said that a lot of the children either moved away from the parish or felt that Catholic school was too strict and transferred to public schools. I was still surprised to see that the number of children was considerably less than the first-grade mob.

The nuns started the day off in the same fashion, ringing a large handheld school bell and bellowing out the familiar orders: no talking, make the sign of the cross on your lips, blah, blah, blah. We were then divided into grades as before, and this time, we were marched up Carlisle Street in single file to the School Annex Building. I was somewhat anxious as I had no idea where the two nuns were taking us, maybe to a house of torture. I felt this way as the nuns were very scary in those black and white outfits since they never broke a smile.

We arrived at the School Annex Building. This was the first time that I was made aware that a classroom existed away from the main school buildings. The nun in charge divided us into two groups, the first floor, and the second floor. We entered the building and were seated in alphabetical order. The setting was completely strange to me, having a classroom in a residential house. The daily classroom instructions were basically the same as first grade, but more intense. Morning prayers, pledge allegiance to the flag, catechism instruction both morning and afternoon, bible study, math, spelling, reading, geography, and my first introduction to poetry.

The school day began with the meeting of all grades in the schoolyard, the area between the school and the nuns' convent. The nun would ring the handheld bell and say, "Silence, get in line." Since we were assigned to the School Annex Building, we were marched single file out of the schoolyard and to the School Annex Building. All along the way, the nun would bark out, "Silence, no talking, make the sign of the cross on your lips." This daily verbiage became annoying and unsettling. Apparently, we were being treated like a herd of lemmings being led by an evil taskmaster.

Since the School Annex Building was located in an older row house, there were a lot of surprises in the school day. Especially in the winter months. There were times when the lock on the door was frozen, and the nun would have to send one of the children back to the main school building to find the maintenance man and tell him the problem. We would all then be standing outside. The heater in the basement would fail. You would sit at your desk, trying to focus on our class work when your fingers were getting numb and you could see your breath as you spoke. At least once, we left the School Annex Building due to a broken furnace, and we all marched back to the main school building and went into the Chapel to continue our classroom day.

When there was snow on the ground, the school day took on a whole new meaning. Of course there was snow in the schoolyard; this made the morning assembly a trip to hell! The nun in charge would holler out, "Do not touch the snow, no one touches the snow" and "Form up into your assigned groups, and silence, no talking, and make the sign of the cross on your lips." We would then be marched out of the schoolyard toward the School Annex Building. The nun with us would also holler out, "Do not touch the snow, stay in a straight line, silence, no talking, make the sign of the cross on your lips." Reaching the School Annex Building, a real shit show would start: kids trying to take off their snow boots, heavy coats, hats, and mittens, all the time being told, "Keep silent, no talking. "The routine would repeat at the end of the school day as we put our winter garb back on, and there was always someone who couldn't find their mittens that they just had in the morning. A return march in the snow back to the main schoolyard for dismissal. The Christmas caroling celebration continued with the handout of the Dairy Maid box of candies. I remember my mother lecturing me before I left for school that morning, "You bring that box of candy home to me, don't you dare open it." When I arrived home with the candy, the ritual of my mother squeezing the chocolate treats continued. That was two years that I did not enjoy any of MY Christmas chocolates.

As I have previously mentioned, we were exposed to intense religious instructions in preparation for our Confirmation by a bishop. This occurred in mid-April after Easter that year. My mother took my white Communion suit to some lady in our neighborhood and had the added material removed and fitted to my grown size. My mother was incapable of sewing on a missing button on a shirt, which wound up being my father's job. She still had to purchase new white shoes and socks as my feet grew and couldn't wear last year's shoes. The previous year's white shirt was a little tight in the collar, and I struggled. We were all prepared and instructed by the nuns that the bishop would select children in church to answer his questions regarding the Sacrament of Confirmation and our faith in the teachings of the Church. I was not called on by the bishop, and really didn't care either.

Parents were invited to the Church to witness the Confirmation of the children. Flashbulbs went off, and, of course, my mother did not have a flash attachment on the Kodak Brownie Camera with the black and white film. Just like first grade, I wore the same white suit in the May Procession, and that was the swan song for that suit, never to be altered again! Second grade also ended with good grade marks and being promoted to third grade. Hold onto your hats, because third grade is when the shit will hit the fan!

September 1957

Third Grade, Age 8

Starting in the later part of second grade and over the summer before entering third grade, I was becoming more aware of what was occurring at home. My eyes were opened to the activities of both my mother and father, which occurred on a daily basis. I finally noticed that my mother was a big smoker. She had a cigarette in her mouth almost all day long. When she finished her "ciggie" as she called it, she would throw the butt in the kitchen sink and run water on it. There were glass ashtrays in every room of the house, but she did not use any of them. This infuriated my father when he came home from work. He would holler at her, "God dammit Irene, stop throwing the butts in the sink, because I have to clean them out." She apparently ignored him as the same routine replayed the next day and the next day, and on and on.

    I also noticed that both my mother and father sat in front of the small black and white TV set every night, drinking beer from bottles. My father would take his empty beer bottle in the kitchen and put it in the beer bottle case. Back then, my mother would call the beer distributor "Belfield Beer Distributor," located two blocks from the house, and have a case of beer delivered. The beer of choice at the time was an old Philadelphia favorite, Ortliebs. The delivery truck would show up the next day, dropping off the full case of beer, and take away the case with the empties. I remember beer being delivered twice a week! My mother, on the other hand, would put her empty beer bottles on the floor next to the sofa where she sat at night. I can vividly remember coming down in the mornings and counting four to five empty beer bottles next to the sofa where she sat. This vision is with me today.

I remember my mother saying that we were going to visit a friend of her mother's, who lived in a section called Mayfair. Never hearing of this place before, I thought that I was going on a long journey. It was during the week, so we walked down to Wyoming Avenue and waited for and then boarded the "trackless trolley" bus, which then took us to 5th Street and Wyoming Avenue. We walked up to Roosevelt Boulevard, where we boarded a bus that went on the Boulevard for what I thought for hours. After a passing of time, my mother said that we were getting off at the next stop. We got off the bus, I don't remember what the name of the street was, but we walked on for several blocks down a tree-lined street.

Finally, we reached our destination and walked up steps to a house that was completely different than our house on 15th Street. My mother rang the doorbell, and a small old lady opened the door. The old lady spoke in a funny voice and said, "Come, come in, I am so excited to see you." I later found out that she was from Ireland and spoke in very heavy brogue. This old woman was very scary to look at, especially for a small child like me. We entered the house, and immediately she grabbed my skinny, little arm and said in her strange voice, "Come over here and put your ass in this chair, and if you get up, 'tis the back of me hand that you'll get." I remember being scared to death:, *is this old bitch going to kill me*! My mother and this lady then went into the kitchen, and I could see them sitting at the kitchen table and talking. I guess that they had something to drink and eat–but I didn't. Eventually my mother came over to where I was sitting. I was told to get up, and we left. I was even afraid to ask if I could go to the bathroom before we left. We walked to the bus, and I said nothing about this strange old woman. I can close my eyes today and remember the old witch's face.

The new school year was a repeat of the previous two years. A big difference was that I was allowed to walk to and from school on my own. WOW I felt like a BFD at the time. We gathered outside in the schoolyard, talking with our classmates and reliving our summer experiences, good or bad as they were. The nun would come out and ring the big handheld school bell. Again, yelling out, "Get in line, no talking, silence, make the sign of the cross on your lips." There were three third grade classrooms with approximately sixty-five kids in each room. I guess that some new kids moved into the parish over the summer. We again were seated in alphabetical order.

The nun this year was short, about five feet. On the first day, she acted completely different than the nuns from the previous two years. The nuns in first and second grade were calm, and more understanding, not as brash. This little penguin came on as a firecracker on the first day! She demanded complete silence and obedience to her, every minute of every day. She would walk up and down the aisles between the desks, carrying her yardstick with her. When she caught anyone talking, she would beat that boy with the yardstick, unmerciful. OH, by the way, she only beat the boys; I never saw her yell at or hit any of the girls in the room. I remember her almost running down the aisles, grabbing a boy by his ear, dragging him to the front of the room, and slamming him to the blackboard. You would actually hear a muffled *crack* from his head hitting the blackboard. I think about this today and wonder how many minor concussions occurred. This penguin dwarf must have been on the rag permanently, as she never once acted in an amicable manner to the boys in the room.

The lessons consisted of religion instructions twice a day, history, spelling, arithmetic, geography, English, and more introduction to poetry. We would read the poems from a book of poetry, then, as a homework assignment, were told to memorize stanza after stanza. The next day the nun would call on people to recite what they memorized. We never discussed what the words of the poem were trying to say. As young as I was, this foray into memorizing poetry for the sake of repeating the words turned me against poetry. I do not partake in poetry in any way, shape, or form today due to this abomination.

During the spelling lessons, we were encouraged to learn the spelling of words and use them properly in sentences. I vividly remember spelling the word "together" in class one day. The nun asked if there were other "hidden words" to be found in the word "together." I raised my hand and she called on me. I said, "Sister" (the rule was to address the nun as "Sister," and if you didn't, you would receive a visit from the yardstick), "There are three words in 'together,' to-get-her."

The nun responded, "You are correct."

A girl sitting close to the front of the room said, "Sister, I will go to-get-her." The nun responded, "Oh my goodness, that is so wonderful." I said to myself, *what a little shithead and suck ass*. The nuns always favored the girls, not the boys in every aspect. From third grade on, the nuns would talk about the "pagan babies" during lent. They would constantly say, "Pray for the pagan babies." Who, what, and where are these babies? I never heard of them being mentioned by my mother and father as big news articles. I never heard the priest at church on Sunday saying, "Pray for the pagan babies." Another line of BS from the nuns just to get into your head.

In third grade I was able to join the church-sponsored Cub Scouts. I thought this was cool, but my mother put up a big stink as she had to buy the Cub Scout uniform for me—*oh*, she had to spend money on something other than beer. The scout meetings were in the church basement on Friday nights, lasting only about one hour. There were Cub Scouts meetings once a week at the scout houses, rotating from boy to boy. It was nice to meet at someone's house and see how other families functioned. The den mothers would serve cupcakes, pretzels, and Kool-Aid to drink. When the meeting came to my house, I hated it. My mother would direct the other boys to sit, and no running around the house, no hollering as my father was watching a western on the TV. There would be stale pretzels, no chips, put out in bowls and water to drink. Couldn't wait for the evening to end.

That year, construction began on the "new school building." The ground behind several of the nuns' convents was used for the new building. The construction caused havoc as a large portion of the schoolyard was used in the construction process.

I was allowed to have a small Halloween party at the house this year. I was able to buy orange and black crepe paper to decorate the living room. I had the traditional black cat cardboard cut-out and a hinged cardboard skeleton. I decorated the living room in anticipation of the upcoming Halloween party. Those familiar with living in a Catholic parish in the city during the 50s are familiar with the "annual block collection by a parish priest." I was home after school in the afternoon, and the doorbell rang. It was the priest for the block collection. My mother opened the door, and the priest came in; it was Father Walsh (remember this name for a fourth grade debacle). The priest came in and spoke to my mother, asking how she was doing, which immediately opened the floodgates. My mother began to weep, pointing to the crepe streamers in the living room ceiling and saying, "My nerves, my nerves, I can't stand this."

Father Walsh looked at me and said "Richard, look at your crying mother, take all of this down now." I balked for a minute but pulled all of the decorations down and let them fall to the floor. There was NO Halloween party now at the house, only a trick-or-treat excursion in the neighborhood.

Halloween was always special to me, with the costumes and free candy. When you were little, your mother went to the local Woolworths or Kresge's and purchased a cheap, simple costume that was in a box. The costume was always a cartoon character that was appearing on the TV at that time. You went from house to house in your neighborhood and on Broad Street (the main street in our neighborhood). You would fill up your goodie bag with treats that would last for weeks. You would get small candy bars, apples, oranges, cookies, gum, taffies, and pennies. I was able to stay up a little later since the next day was All Saints Day, a holy day and a day off from school– but you had to attend a special children's mass at the church. As I went to bed on Halloween, my mother told me, "Make sure you are asleep by midnight as the dead will be coming out of their graves tonight." WOW, let's really scare the little kid. I remember clearly her saying that to me.

The Christmas ritual repeated itself again, "Don't you dare open that box of candy, bring it directly home to me," and the candy squeezing began. So far for three years now, I did not have any of my Christmas candy.

At the end of the year, I had good grades and was promoted to the fourth grade. I looked back and recounted several times when the little nun from another world broke at least two ward sticks on my back. As my mother had previously said, "The sisters don't hit you unless you did something wrong." In my mother's eyes, the nuns never did anything wrong, as they were messengers of God. The last day of school presented a rather novel experience. The nun called out many of the children in the room and asked them to stand up. The nun would say, "Oh, little Mary, you get a holy card for being so religious during the school year," and "Little Susan, you get a holy card for helping Sister in the class during the year," and it went on and on, holy cards for spelling, neatness, etc. The penguin nun called out my name and told me to stand up. "Richard Etherton, you win the award for the worst handwriting in the room." WOW, you little dwarf, talk about hurting a small child's feelings–what a loser! This adds to the reason why I have very little respect for the nuns today.

My mother did not drive, as she kept saying her nerves were too bad. Thank God she didn't, as we would probably would have had numerous accidents with her at the wheel. My father was, therefore, the chauffeur, driving her at a moment's whim. My mother was always trying to "suck up" to the nuns (sisters, as she called them). Twice a year she would have my father drive her to Parisis Pizza on the 5100 block of 5th Street. She would order two large pizza pies, telling the pizza maker, "Make sure they are well cooked, a little burnt on the edge." By the way, my mother cooked everything at home "burnt or well-done," as she would say. She would then have my dad drive her to the back of the nuns' convents on Carlisle Street and she would ring the doorbell. She would have me stand there with her as the nun would answer the door. My mother would then ask for Sister So-And-So (whoever the nun was that I currently had in school), and when Sister So-And-So would show up, my mother would introduce herself as "Richard's mother," as I stood there looking like a complete little asshole.

My mother and the nun would exchange pleasantries, and my mother would go into a long dissertation about how she was a graduate of West Philly High School for Girls, and that she grew up in South Philly and was a member of the King of Peace Catholic Parish at 26th and Wharton Streets, blah, blah, blah. The nun would acknowledge, as I was in her class, and offer thanks for the two pizzas and reenter the convent. This showboat would occur on a Friday evening. Getting back into the car, we drove home, and nothing was said about this off-Broadway play. My mother would explain later that this "act of kindness to the sisters would be remembered in heaven." *Ok, if you say so*. I think that she was trying to buy some preferential treatment for me in school. Guess what, IT DIDN'T WORK! The same nun that took the pizzas was the same nun on Monday who would smack me in the back with her yardstick, and for no real reason, just because she felt like hitting the boys in the room.

Sister Schmuck drove into our heads on Friday afternoons that because we had made both our First Communion and Confirmation, we must go to Confession every Saturday so we could receive the Eucharist on Sunday morning. Going to Confession every Saturday afternoon was a chore. At this young age, what major sins had you committed since last Saturday's Confession? You started to make up shit to tell the priest in the confessional. All of us kids felt the same way.

I told my mother that the nun (Sister) said that we should read passages from the Bible with our parents on a weekly basis. My mother said, "Do not read the Bible, there is nothing there that you should know about." I never told the nun what my mother said for fear of being hit by the nun.

As I had stated earlier, the nuns would check the kids' envelopes to verify which child was at Sunday Mass. We sat together as a grade, but the nuns had to absolutely verify that you were in church on Sunday and that it wasn't a doppelganger. My parents would give me ten or fifteen cents (this was 1957) to put in my envelope and make sure that I put my name on the outside of the envelope so I would get credit for being in church. I remember one Monday morning in school, the little dwarf nun called up a little girl to the front of the room. She started to holler at the girl, "You do not put pennies in your church envelope, GOD does not want pennies, you do not give pennies to GOD." Why you little ignorant runt of a nun, did you ever think that the child might come from a large family and this is all her parents had to give her for the collection basket?

As I have said several times, these nuns had no concept of family life with the children. I remember a little boy who sat in the row as I did, about three seats behind me. This little guy was always singing little silly songs quietly so the nun did not hear him. One day he unexpectedly sang a tune a little louder, "push in the button, pull out my chain, out comes a chocolate cho cho train." He probably heard this little ditty from an older brother. Well, the nun heard this and actually flew down the aisle, grabbed this little guy by the hair, and threw him against the back wall. The boy got up, crying hysterically, and the nun slapped him again and again. She told him to go to Mother Superior's office and tell her what he was singing. The little guy didn't come back to school for two days.

Since I had made both my Communion and Confirmation, my mother believed that I should attend church with her during the summer months. We would attend mass every Sunday as a family, and on the first Fridays, just the two of us. The church was not air-conditioned, as almost all of the old-style churches were not. Being a little kid, I would be squirming around in the pew as mass was being conducted. You could wear shorts and a decent top to Mass during the week over the summer period. My mother would actually pinch my legs and say, "Stop moving around, be still, be quiet, pay attention to the priest." Little kids squirm around, no matter where they are, church or at home. My mother would always be telling me, "Sit down, stop moving around, be still," I would hear this on a repeated basis no matter where I was. I remember my mother saying that she was going to have me checked for worms since I couldn't sit still. Kids are only little once, and this is how they act.

Every Saturday, per the nuns' directions, I had to go to Confession. My mother, father, and I would go to Confession, then to a bar to eat sandwiches and drink beer until seven or eight, then go home. Going to Confession every Saturday when you are little is ridiculous. You start to make shit up to tell the priest. At this age, how many banks did you rob or push old ladies down the stairs, or how many people did you kill?

My mother's drinking and smoking continued. At this young age, I could determine when my mother was hit in the ass. She would walk and stumble around, slur her words, have this goofy look on her face, and always have her "ciggie" in her mouth. I was bothered by her actions then and as I remember them now.

September 1958

Fourth Grade, Age 9

Fourth grade started in the same manner as had the previous three grades. There were three fourth-grade rooms, where we were again marched to our new classrooms with the same BS "Silence, no talking, make the sign of the cross on your lips." We were seated again in alphabetical order.

I heard stories about the fourth-grade nun that I was assigned to. She was portrayed as a real sweetheart in the totally opposite of the words meaning. She had a nickname as "Sister Tommy Gun." It didn't take very long to find out why she was called this. The second or third day of the new school year proved her hate for boys in full color. One of the boys did something wrong and Sister Tommy Gun went into full attack mode. Tommy Gun literally ran down the aisle to the little boy's desk, grabbed him by the ear (the usual mode of operation), and dragged him to the front of the room. She told the boy to stand still–don't move. She began to slap his face with both of her hands in a very fast manner truly sounding like a tommy (machine) gun. She said to the little boy, "Go home and tell your mother that your cheeks were on the frying pan." The boy returned to his desk, and as he walked down the aisle, I noticed his cheeks were blood red.

This act of vengeance by Tommy Gun was played out throughout the year in almost regular weekly reoccurrence. As I stated before, the nuns took their frustrations out on only the boys in the class. I can never remember that any of these nuns hit, smacked, or pushed any of the girls in the classrooms. These women had hatred in both their hearts and minds and had no problem displaying their feelings toward the boys in the rooms. I told my mother about Tommy Gun and she hollered at me, saying, "Don't ever give one of the good sisters a nickname." I was smart enough to not tell my mother when Tommy Gun went on a rampage. When Tommy Gun left the classroom, she would select one of her favorite, special little girls to "watch the room when she was out, and to take names of any talking or playing around." When Tommy Gun returned, she took vengeance on any boy whose name was on the list–there was never a girl name was on the list. More BS.

The curriculum in fourth grade followed the same outlines as previous grades, except more of everything. More catechism. Math, geography, history, English, spelling, Bible history, and, yes, more BS poetry. Memorizing the poems and reciting them in class–what a waste of time. I started to notice that some of the children, both boys and girls, were slow learners. That is to say, they didn't totally grasp some of the lessons as easily as the other students. These poor children would be identified today as "learning disabled." They did not receive any special treatment or individual help from the "wonderful nuns." These poor kids fell between the cracks in the floor and were labeled by the nun as troublemakers. The nun told these children to "get a tutor at home." This was the only salvation if their parents had the financial basis to afford a tutor at home. Personally, I knew of no child who was tutored at home; parents had a hard enough time putting clothes on the child and food on the tables.

I remember in catechism class, which occurred both mornings and afternoons, the nun was talking about heaven, and how the Church perceived it would be. When one of the little girls asked, "What will we do in heaven if we get there?"

The nun said, "The Church teaches that we will enjoy the beatifical vision of GOD." She went on to say, "Our enjoyment will be seeing GOD the Father in all of his majesty." Silence overtook the classroom for a few minutes, and a little boy raised his hand and asked the nun, "Are there sports in heaven, like baseball and football, what are we going to do all day, how about TV to watch the Roy Rogers show?"

Well, ole Tommy Gun went into a hysterical rant, "How dare you blaspheme and question the Church teachings? The Church teaches doctrine and you will not question it." She then proceeded down the aisle to the little boy and started to smack him about the head and face. Finally she retreated to the front of the classroom and continued to preach the teachings of the catechism. What a shmuck, the little boy just asked a logical question from a small child's mind, show compassion, you ignorant penguin.

I told my mother about what happened with the little boy's question. My mother said, "Don't ever question the good Sister, she is there to teach you religion and about GOD."

One day in early September, the self-proclaimed music nun came into my classroom. She said that she was there to select new members of the church choir. She stood at the front of the room and pointed to four of the boys and said, "You, you, you, and you are in the choir." Guess what, I was one of the suckers selected. There was no consideration given if you could carry a tune.

We were hustled out of the classroom and down the stairs, all the time being told, "Silence, no talking, put the sign of the cross on your lips." We were led through a back door into the chapel, where we were introduced to Professor Bansbach, the choir leader. He told us that we would being singing in the church choir at all of the major church celebrations: Christmas, Easter, Holy Days, High Mass, etc. The music nun (who had a loud squeaking voice that sounded like a cat's tail stuck under a rocking chair) told us that we should consider us to be blessed to be in the choir. The professor then wanted to hear our voices repeating a scale of musical notes. All of us, including me, SUCKED. We were not singers, or candidates for any church choir. After struggling for about thirty minutes, the Professor told us that every Wednesday at 11:00 a.m., a message would come over the intercom in each room directing the "choir members to meet in the

Chapel." Choir practice ran from 11:00 a.m. to noon, when the church bell would ring. You then had to hurry home, inhale your lunch, and rush back to school so as not to be late for the afternoon session. When I told my mother that I was in the choir, she exclaimed, "You are so blessed to be in the choir, this is wonderful, so wonderful, I can't wait to call your Aunt Ann and tell her, such a blessing." I had to hear this over and over.

The next week we meet for the first time with all of the other choir members from the higher grades for choir practice. We were grouped according to our grades and ages. This being my first time in this type of setting, I was overwhelmed. The choir practice started with singing (or trying to sing) various hymns for Sunday mass. For those not familiar with the Catholic Church at that time, the entire mass was in Latin, and the Priest did not face the congregation during the mass. The choir would sing most of the hymns in Latin and respond to the priest in Latin. Talk about throwing the kitchen sink at a small child, along with their regular studies in the classroom!

The Sunday routine was to go the children's mass at 9:00 a.m., which usually finished up at 10:00 a.m. unless the priest went on an extended roll preaching from the pulpit, rush home after mass, gobble up/inhale your breakfast, do your business in the bathroom, hurry up and get back to church to sing in the choir for the 11:00 a.m. High Mass, which finished around 12:15 p.m. You wore a black cassock which was furnished by the church. Your parents had to purchase the white surplus top which had to be washed and heavily starched every week. You also had to purchase the white celluloid collar and collar button. My mother had no problem buying these items since it was for church. The nun in charge of the choir at the High Mass would tie these big stupid black bows around the collar. We would then go from the back of the chapel to the main church through a back entrance behind the main altar and wait until the Professor began to play the huge church organ. We would then come out of our "hiding place" from behind the main altar and move halfway down the center aisle, stop, and start singing an entrance hymn. When finished, we would go to the vestibule area in the entrance area of the church and go up these small twisting stairs to the choir loft. The nun would be with us constantly saying, "Silence, no talking." We would take our places on the steps in the choir loft. I was surprised to see that the choir included six or seven men who would join in with us in singing throughout the mass. When mass was over, we had to wait for the congregation to clear out in the vestibule, so we could go back to the chapel area and remove our choir outfits. We would get home after 1:00 p.m., with not much of the Sunday remaining for "me time." This ritual occurred every Sunday from mid-September until mid-May of the following year, two times to church every Sunday.

Let me tell you about Christmas. We had to sing at the 5:30 a.m. High Mass, (how cruel is it to get a small child up before 5:00 a.m. on Christmas morning), attend the 9:00 a.m. children's mass, and come back again to sing at the 11:00 a.m. High Mass. How about screwing up a small child's Christmas morning and half of the day.

Palm Sunday required us to get up before the chickens to sing at the High Mass at 5:30 a.m., wrap up 7:00 a.m., go home, eat breakfast, then go to the children's mass at 9:00 a.m., go home, then come back to sing at the 11:00 a.m. High Mass.

Let's look at Easter. Our Easter holiday at school started on the Wednesday before Easter Sunday. The choir would then have to sing at the 7:00 p.m. High Mass in the church on Holy Thursday evening, which would wrap up around 9:00 p.m. We would then sing for three hours of agony on Good Friday, which went from noon until 3:00 p.m. We had to be at the chapel by 11:30 a.m. and we would leave around 3:30 p.m. Next came Holy Saturday, and we would have to sing at the High Mass, starting around 7:00 p.m. and ending up around 9:00 p.m. Easter Sunday was a repeat of Palm Sunday the week before, 5:30 a.m. High Mass, 9:00 a.m. children's mass, 11:00 a.m. High Mass.

Easter Monday was the ONLY day off from church, then Tuesday back to school, where the other children had all of that time off, some even taking little local trips with their families. If you missed singing in the choir, you'd better have a damn good reason; your mother had to write a detailed excuse note to the choir nun explaining in the greatest detail why you missed singing in the choir. My mother said this was the greatest event in my life to be singing in the choir and attending all of these mass celebrations. The choir routine extended all the way into eighth grade. When I graduated from eighth grade, I also graduated from the choir madness. My mother kept saying, "What a wonderful blessing on you, being in the choir." OK, remind me of that as the next few years approached.

Halloween came again that year. My mother reminded me again when I came home from trick or treat, "Get in bed and go to sleep. Remember the dead come out of their graves after midnight." Why scare a small child saying this again! I asked some of my friends if their moms warned them of the "Halloween dead" and they all laughed at me and said I was nuts.

The Christmas holiday came around, and so did the Dairy Maid candy box ritual, "Don't you open that box of candy, bring it straight home to me," and the chocolate squeezing continued. Another year that I did not enjoy my Christmas box of candy.

The nuns would march us out of the classrooms at both lunchtime and dismissal. We would be placed into lines outside the classrooms and then led down the stairs outside to formations leading to four different directions, usually led by two nuns, constantly barking out, "Silence, no talking, stay in line, put the sign of the cross on your lips." In the winter months, we would also hear, "Do not touch the snow, no one is to touch the snow." Eight years of this constant BS!

Remember Father Walsh, who forced me to take down the Halloween decorations in third grade? Well here we go at it again. In the spring, my mother had some wild idea in her head that she wanted to scare the neighbors on 15th Street and be a "blockbuster." That was an expression at that time to signify that you would be the first family on your block to sell to a black family.

My mother was not as religious as she thought she was, or as religious as she wanted other people to think so. My mother had a mean side to her which, when brought out into the open, was horrifying. My mother could be happy and friendly to you and could turn on you in a heartbeat. She would always look for a reason to start an argument with you or anyone who was with you– and for no apparent reason. I witnessed her start arguments with both neighbors, close friends, and relatives. My mother was only happy when she was arguing with someone.

For reasons, only known to her, she wanted to piss off our neighbors and make a stupid point. Our neighborhood and Holy Child Parish was lily white in the spring of 1959. There were no black, brown, or oriental families in our immediate location. My mother wanted to "put a scare in the people," as she so eloquently said. She had my father invite one of the black workers who reported to him at the Philadelphia Water Department. The plan was to have this man and his wife and children come up to our house on a Sunday afternoon. The time arrived, and I was outside; it was a sunny, warm day, so several of our neighbors were outside on their porches. The gentleman showed up in a big car (maybe a Buick or Oldsmobile), and he brought his wife and three children. The ages of the children ranged from about six to twelve years. The whole family was dressed to the extremes: a derby on the father, some type of a fur coat on the wife, and the children were dressed better than I ever was. They parked the big car in our driveway, and when they got out of the vehicle, the side show started.

The father came up on our porch and rang the doorbell, and my father came out on the porch to meet him. My mother joined him, and the both of them started to talk up our house, the driveway, and the garage, the "nicest part of our house." The entire family came into our house, and I followed them. My parents bonded with this family immediately, telling them about the church and school in our parish. They were escorted through our house and looked in every bedroom, kitchen, and dining room. My father took everyone into the basement to look at the new gas heater. The family went outside, and my mother walked them up the driveway to see the garage, all the while talking about how nice our house was and how great it would be to live in this neighborhood. All this time several of our neighbors were outside on their porches watching and listening to this charade. Eventually the family got back into their car and drove away. My mother called to me to come into the house and sit down on the sofa. She began to tell me this was an act to scare the neighbors into thinking that "we were going to sell to blacks." I asked why, and I was told that it was not my business to know why, but she was doing this.

That night the shit storm started. Our phone began to ring and when my mother picked up the receiver, the other party hung up the phone. This act started in the late afternoon and continued all through the night. The phone would ring constantly, and no one was on the other end. My mother would holler into the phone, "Who are you? Stop calling, stop, I will call the police." The phones at this time were all hard-wired into the small connection box in your house. There was no phone jack to disconnect your phone as there is today. My mother eventually left the receiver off the phone cradle, and the phone calls stopped but the phone made loud chirping sounds all night long. We had only one phone in the dining room, and you could hear the noise all the way upstairs. I closed my bedroom door to get some sleep. The next day was Monday, and my mother said she was going to walk up to the Bell Telephone office at Broad and Rockland Streets. She was going to complain about the annoying phone calls and have our phone number changed. WAIT A MINUTE HERE: you started the shit with the people coming to the house to put on your little show, and you are going to complain about annoying phone calls?

I went around to my friend's house, as usual, so we could walk to school together. When I knocked on the front door, I was told that "he left for school already." This was strange as we always went to school together. When I got to school, as soon as I walked into the classroom, ole Tommy Gun called me to the front of the room and said, "You are in the hot seat today." I then went to my desk and sat down, wondering what the old bag was talking about. It didn't take very long for the story to start to formulate. After morning prayers and pledge allegiances to the flag,

Mother Superior came to the front door of the classroom. She said something to Tommy Gun and I was called to the front of the room. Mother Superior told me to come with her to her office. Visions of torture came into my head, as I had no idea of what was going to happen, what did I do? I followed her into her office, and she sat down, telling me to stand at the doorway. She started by telling me that the parish did not appreciate what my parents were trying to accomplish. She then told me to go over to the rectory and that Father Walsh (remember this jerk from last year at Halloween) would be waiting for me.

I took my cost from the cloakroom, walked down the stairs of the school building, and walked over to the rectory building. I went up to the huge front door of the rectory and knocked. An elderly lady answered the door and told me to go into the room and wait for Father Walsh. I waited for what seemed like an hour, and Father Walsh came into the room and sat down at a large desk. He stared at me with what seemed like hate and fire in his eyes. Finally he spoke, "The monsignor and the parish are aware of what occurred at your house yesterday." He opened a drawer in the desk, handed me an envelope and said, " Take this letter home and hand it to your mother immediately, do not stop on the way and talk to no one, do you understand me ?"

I immediately said, "Yes, Father."

Father Walsh then said, "You are a troublemaker because of this."

I left the rectory and walked home very fast. I knocked on our door and rang the doorbell (my mother didn't trust me with a door key, saying that I would lose it and someone could come in to rob us. Trust me, we had nothing worthy of being stolen). My mother came to the door and said, "What are you doing home now, did something happen at school?" I handed her the letter from Father Walsh; she opened it and spent a few minutes reading and digesting it. She looked at me and said "Go back to school." I asked what was in the letter, but my mother said it was not any of my business. She never told me what was in that letter until I asked her about ten years later. She said, "The parish monsignor asked me to reconsider my actions and not to be a blockbuster," which meant not to be the first family to sell their house to a black family.

I returned to school and the real shit show started. I came into the classroom, and ole Tommy Gun looked at me with fire in her eyes and probably hate in her heart. I went to my desk and sat down. The kids around me looked at me as if I had just killed someone. About an hour into my return, Tommy Gun said, "We will have a desk check now." A desk check consisted of you taking all of the books out of your desk and placing them on the top of your desk. The nun would come down the aisle and randomly pick a student and then go through their books, looking for torn or missing pages, pencil marks on the pages, corners of the pages turned over, books not covered, etc. This poor excuse of a person walked down the aisle and stopped at my desk. She started going through my books. She found torn pages, pencil scribbling on various pages, corners of pages folded over or torn off. She began to smack me with a wooden ruler that she carried in her pocket, saying. "You bold, brazen article, who do you think you are, defacing schoolbook property" and "You will stay after school today and think of what you did."

The issue is, I didn't deface my books; the kids around me must have when I left the classroom to go to the rectory and take the letter home. I even remember one little girl having one of my books that was originally in my desk and took the book up to Tommy Gun. This turd of a nun hollered at me again, saying, "More destruction of schoolbooks." I sat after school that day and erased most of the pencil scribblings in my books. Finally Tommy Gun told me to get up from my desk and go home, and tell my mother what I did. When I got home, my mother wanted to know where I was and why I was late coming home. I told her about my books being defaced and that I didn't do it, and that the nun (Sister) smacked me several times with her wooden ruler."

My mother said, "Well, you must have done something wrong, as the good Sister would not have hit you for nothing." Again, I took the fall for something that I did not cause, especially on that day. My parents always took the side of the priest and the nun; in their minds; the priest and nun could do no wrong.

I had to go to the dentist for the filling of a cavity filling. The dentist was located in a building on the second floor of Broad and Rockland Streets. The receptionist at the dentist was the older daughter of a neighbor. I had to fill out the paperwork, which, of course, included my address and phone number. Guess how the phone number got passed along the street. My mother had the phone number changed again, and it took only two days for the neighbors to get the new phone number, and the annoyance calls started again, day and night. The phone number would be changed more than five times until my mother paid the extra money and got a private, unlisted line from Bell Telephone. My neighborhood friends were very cold toward me, to the point of avoidance. Classmates also kept their distance from me for several weeks. Old friendships didn't return until the end of the school year and summertime. I still felt that bad feelings were there.

The school year ended with the repeat of the previous year, holy cards and kudos and kind words to other children in the classroom, and I was singled out again, standing up and being told, "And you get the award for the worst handwriting in the room." These nuns really knew how to break down a child's self-esteem. Promoted to the fifth grade with passing grades, nothing exceptional. Sister Shmuck handed out a summer reading list, consisting of books for girls! The list was *Little Women*, *Pippi Longstocking*, *Heide Grows Up*, and so on. NOT one book geared toward a young boy's reading desires.

The drinking and smoking continued at home, sometimes really kicked up a notch or two.

That summer my mother and father said, "We are going to look for a new house so we can move away from this lousy neighborhood." WOW, what a comment. Our search had to be within the Philadelphia City limits as was required by my father's job. We looked at a few new homes identified as "sample houses." I was so excited when I walked into a new single house; it was something that I never experienced before in my life. The new house was so amazing and big, with no clutter in the rooms and a modern kitchen (which we did not have on 15th Street), at least two bathrooms, with a shower (which we did not have on 15th Street), and a house smell that I had never experienced before.

My mother went from room to room complaining that "the rooms are smaller than my house now."

My father would say, "The house isn't built strong enough." On and on, they would talk, both condemning the new house that was completely superior to where we were living now. This was a single home with a nice lawn and backyard in a new neighborhood. The worst memory of house hunting that I had was when we were looking again at a new development. We went into the new house, and, again, I was almost in heaven with the experience. My mother and father went upstairs to look at the bedrooms and bathrooms. I heard my mother say to my father, "Watch and see if anyone is coming up the stairs, I have to use the toilet to pee." I heard the toilet flush a few minutes later and both parents came downstairs. This terrible memory is fused into my head today!

We got in the car, and my mother said, "The new houses aren't any better than our house now." So, we started looking at the houses that had sale signs on the lawns. We would only look at houses that had garages. My father was obsessed with putting his car in the garage. We would drive around on a Sunday afternoon, in different sections of the city. When my mother would see a house that she liked, my father would stop the car and she would get out. She would walk up to the front door and knock/ring the doorbell. Someone would answer the door and I could see my mother talking to the person at the door. She would return to the car and tell my father that the person told her to call the realtor whose name was on the sale sign. The realtor would set up the appointment to see the house. My mother was mad that the person would not even tell her what the asking price was. I later found out that contacting a realtor was the correct thing to do, and not my mother's route. We looked at a few more houses for sale, with the same scenario, my mother going up to the door, ringing the doorbell, talking to the person, and being pissed when told to call the realtor. After a couple of Sundays spent driving around and not getting any information from the homeowners, we stopped looking. My mother said, "None of these houses are better than where we live now, we are staying in our house." And so went the summer of looking for a new house in a better neighborhood.

I remember going to church with my mother during the summer months. There would be little children and babies crying and fussing around, as little ones do. My mother would say to me, "Why are these kids here? They should be left home, I can't think of my prayers, they are a distraction." WOW, even at a young age I knew this was not how to address this.

September 1959

Fifth Grade, Age 10

The school year started off in the same fashion as previous years. Seeing old friends and classmates and hoping for a better school year with no BS from the penguins. The old nun rang the school bell and called out, "Silence, get in line, no talking, put the sign of the cross on your lips." Sounds like the same old storyline to me.

We were told to get into different groups according to this year's grades. Much to my surprise, I was assigned to a fifth grade LAY Teacher, Miss Mary. This would be the first time that I did not have a nun teaching me–what a relief. Miss Mary was the only Lay Teacher in our school. We went up the steps in the old school building and into our classroom. There was an entirely different feeling in the classroom, one of a relaxed atmosphere. Miss Mary taught all the subjects except religion. When religion time was on the list, a girl was sent to one of the other classrooms to bring back a nun who taught religion and Bible study to us. With the nun in the room, animosity was in the air, and you could feel it. When she finished and left the room, things returned to normal. Any discipline issues were first addressed by Miss Mary, and if she failed, a nun would be called in and the culprit(s) would be removed from the room and taken to the corridor. You could hear the shouting, hollering, and smacking of the child by the Gestapo nun. The child would return to the room with a red face and probably hurt feelings. Again, I never saw one of the girls in the classroom singled out for disciplinary measures.

I somewhat enjoyed fifth grade, with geography, U.S. history, and math, but there was still my outright hate for poetry. Why did we have to memorize such stupid words and messages buried in sentences that meant absolutely nothing? I remember talking to my friends who went to public school, about the various school trips that the school took them on. They went to see the Liberty Bell, Independence Hall, the Philadelphia Mint, Museum of Art, etc. The parochial school system did not get involved with school trips for the students. The philosophy was that the students' parents were responsible for trips outside the school's teachings. The problem was that my parents were not open to taking me to those places of interest, so I missed out.

Halloween came and went, with no threats of the dead coming out of their graves to get me. Christmas returned with the same ole message, "Don't you dare open that box of candy, bring it home to me." The choir assignment continued with attending and singing at two masses every Sunday. As I mentioned before, once you were in the choir, there was no getting out unless you dropped dead or moved out of the parish. I moved up from the Cub Scouts to the Boy Scouts that year, with a lot of BS from Mom. She had to spend money to buy the Boy Scout uniform, hat, scarf, sleeping bag, mess hall kits, canteen, and other miscellaneous items. All she did was complain and said, "Is all of this necessary?"

I remember one weekend, our Scout Troop 281 went camping at Camp Charles (named after Reverend Charles McGinley, our parish monsignor), on Route 73, near Mermaid Lane. The trip started off with rain on the morning we started out. My father drove me and three other scouts to the campsite, and my mother accompanied us. We arrived at the campsite to find a muddy landscape, where we were required to unpack tents from a pickup truck and set up the tents in a light rain. We were all soaked to the skin within minutes. I heard my mother talking to the scoutmaster about why we had to be out in the rain and that we should stop. My parents were the only ones there and kept carrying on with the scoutmaster. My father called me over and said that I should leave and come home, I said NO. My mother and father stayed until we had our tent up and went inside our tent for a respite from the rain, which now was a little heavier. I was so embarrassed by the actions of my parents, as some of the other scouts looked at me with grins on their faces. This camp outing was for all of the scouts in our troop, new guys called "tenderfoots" up to Eagle Scouts. Wow, what an impression I made.

The camping trip involved trekking into the woods and looking for all kinds of nature. We were able to change out of our wet uniforms and at least put on dry underwear and socks. The food being prepared by the scout leaders was lousy: baked beans, hot dogs, and Kool-Aid. We had to sleep in our sleeping bags, which, by this time, were wet from the rains. A tough night sleeping in a tent with three other guys and in wet sleeping bags, but we made it to the next morning. The next morning, we had scrambled eggs which tasted like cardboard. We broke down the tents, packed up our gear, and loaded the tents and other camping stuff on the pick-up truck. My father and mother showed up, and me and the other three guys went home. All I heard on the ride home was, "Why did you want to go on this trip with the rainy weather? All of your clothes are wet, you are going to get sick now." The silence in my father's car was deafening. This was the first and last scout camping trip that I went on.

I remember when friends of my parents visited us on a Saturday afternoon. They all had a few beers and were talking BS. My mother called me up from the basement, where I was playing with my trains. My mother said to the people, "Richard is in the choir at church, and he will sing for you." I looked at her and thought, what was I, some kind of sideshow? My mother then said, "Sing for these people," but when I balked, she began to holler, "Sing, sing I tell you." I looked at her and went up to my room and closed the door. The issue was never brought up to me again.

The drinking and smoking were at a new level. My mother was NOT one to cook and prepare a Sunday dinner. She had my father drive her around in different locales. I had to go with them on these escapades.

My mother would say, "Oh look, there is an American Legion/VFW, let's go in and have a few beers." We would enter these places, which smelled like cigarettes, spilled beer, and body odor. We would sit at a table, and my father would bring the beers and a small Coke for me–this then became our Sunday meal. I would eat and sit there like a little asshole with nothing to do. Sometimes we would go to the CPO Club at the Philadelphia Navy Yard on a Sunday afternoon. The same routine would follow: beers, sandwiches, and a glass of Coke, still sitting there like the asshole that I was. I remember one time my mother was so drunk that when we left to go home, she projection-hurled down the steps of the CPO Club. I was so embarrassed!

On occasional Saturdays we would go to the Commissary Store at the Philadelphia Navy Yard. There my parents would buy groceries, dry good items, and two cases of beer (which was cheaper than the cost at the local beer distributor). My mother also bought two or three cartons of ciggies, as they were extremely reasonable since no taxes were being collected. We would start home and stop at the Schmidt's Beer Brewery. This brewery was located off of Girard Avenue around 2nd and 3rd Streets and is not in operation today. We would enter the bar area, which had the smell of spilled beer, cigarette/cigar smoke, and just plain old rotten stink. This place was old, very old, as it was part of the Schmidt's Brewery. There was a distorted tin ceiling that was coming down on a few places, and yes, there were spittoons around the bar. We would sit at a table; my father would get beers for Mom and him and a small glass of Coke for me. He would order sandwiches, which an old woman with very few teeth in her mouth would bring to our table. This old bag looked as old as this bar, and she smelled bad too. SOO, as usual, I would eat my sandwich, drink my soda, and sit there like the little asshole that I was becoming. Eventually we would leave this joint and drive home; the sandwich was my Saturday lunch/supper combination.

I remember during the winter months, my lips became very chapped and looked as if I had a mustache. They burned when I had anything to eat that was hot. Miss Mary, the teacher, noticed the condition and said, "When you go home, ask your mother to let you use ChapStick on your lips to clear up the redness." Remember, this condition was going on for a few days and my mother did not notice it or act to correct it. When I got home, I told my mother what the teacher said to use on my chapped lips. My mother said, she was not going out to buy ChapStick, and that Vaseline was just as good. SOO, here I was, putting Vaseline on my chapped lips because Mother didn't want to buy the ChapStick. I looked like a freak with those shiny lips. Ever since that day, I always make sure that I have ChapStick available to use.

Easter time arrived, and I was subjected to attending and singing at the prescribed rituals of the Easter vigils and masses. My mother kept saying, "This is such a blessing." Remember Father Walsh? Well he said one of the Easter masses, and he noticed me and probably remembered me because he looked at me with a cold, hard stare in his eyes, as if to say "remember me?"

I graduated from fifth grade successfully, with no holy cards being handed out or shaming of my handwriting–what a break! I can look back and say that fifth grade was perhaps the most enjoyable of my eight years at Holy Child Parish School, because there was NO nun lashing out with her BS and hate. I actually walked away from fifth grade knowing that I did learn something, and it was not because of the "good sisters," as my mother would always say.

The week before school started, my mother said that she wanted to go to the Cannstatter in N.E. Philly, somewhere on Academy Road. This was an old German folk festival that ran for three days, ending on Labor Day. We finally found the place after my father got lost a few times since he was not familiar with the N.E. Philly areas. We parked the car and walked into the outdoor festival, and there was a small fee charged. There were picnic benches all around, with a decent crowd of people there. There were these guys dressed in short pants, suspenders, flowery shirts, and funny hats. They were playing strange music (which later I was told were German folk tunes) and there was a short, round little guy blowing into a large tuba and making the strangest sounds that I'd ever heard.

We sat at one of the picnic benches, and my father went to get a pitcher of beer and glasses for him and my mother. He went back and returned with a bottle of Coke for me. Wow, I graduated to a bottle of soda this time. So, we sat for a while, and my father took me with him to the food stand, and he got a large hot dog with sauerkraut, which I later learned was not a large hot dog but a knockwurst. I was allowed to get a hot dog with sauerkraut, and this time mustard! When my mother made hot dogs at home, she would cut mine in half and then serve it to me on a piece of white bread with ketchup on it, not mustard. This was the first time that I had a hot dog on a hot dog bun with mustard and sauerkraut. Boy-o-boy did I enjoy that hot dog. My mother started her shit with me saying, "Why did you get a hot dog, it might not be cooked properly." I pretended not to hear her and just enjoyed the moment with the hot dog on a bun. I had to sit at the picnic table and only get up to go to the bathroom with my father. I saw a few other kids running around and playing with each other; but I was told to sit down and be still. There were people in fancy garb and even the women wore the goofy little hats. There was folk dancing and singing of German songs by the men in the short pants and funny hats. We stayed until it started to get dark, and we drove home. The next day was going to be the first day of school.

September 1960

Sixth Grade, Age 11

The school year started as before, the old nun ringing the school bell and hollering, "Get in lines, no talking, silence, put the sign of the cross on your lips, blah, blah, blah" and "Eighth grade over here, seventh grade over here, sixth grade over here," and so on. I knew that I would be assigned to a classroom with a nun this year, as I had the only lay teacher in fifth grade last year.

This year we were going to be in the new school building with new desks and books. So we marched around the back of the old school building to the entrance of the new school building and up the stairs. The new school building had three floors, and if I remember correctly, we were on the first floor. We went into the assigned classroom. Wow, what a feeling to see new walls, new desks, new blackboards, even a new smell, and all new books. About fifty kids were in the room. I guessed right: we were assigned a nun who had the nickname of "Breatho." All you had to do was to get close to hear as she spoke, and you knew how she got the nickname of "Breatho." Her breath smelled like the bottom of the monkey's cage at the zoo; it really stunk all day, every day.

The school day was basically the same, with religion twice a day in the morning and after lunch. We had geography, math, world history, English, spelling, Bible history, and again, stupid, useless poetry. We were taught in English class how to conjugate a verb and diagram a sentence. What shithole job in hell would require this nonsense as a prerequisite to employment or as a basis to keep your job in the real world? A complete waste of time being taught something, and then being tested on it and graded. Why this BS was taught, I will never understand. This nun said that we should practice our division and multiplication tables at home, especially on the weekends, when we were away from the classroom. OK, what time do we have for ourselves?

This nun wasn't so much for hitting you, just calling you up to the front of the room and screaming in your face until you felt like you were going to throw up from the stink of her breath. Again, I do not remember the nun screaming at any of the girls in the class. This year we were exposed by the nun talking about vocations to the priesthood and sisterhood. The girls were given pamphlets on entering the convents, and the boys were given pamphlets detailing the priesthood and told to take them home to read with our parents. I showed my mother the pamphlet and said that the nun (Sister) said that we should read about the priesthood. My mother read and absorbed the information on the pamphlet as if it were a requirement of life. The school day wasn't too bad this year, except for the screaming and bad breath experiences, which occurred every day. My mother tried the "pizza giveaway" again this school year. Believe me it did not work as she planned it to. This nun was still obnoxious to me in every way she could be. Did my mother honestly believe that she could buy favor with these penguins?

The choir routine continued every Sunday and Holyday/Easter occasion. It was now becoming more and more of a ritual. And my mother continued to tell me, "This is a great blessing on you." My mother now started to harp on me about entering the priesthood: "How great it would be if you became a priest, such a blessing on us, why don't you become a priest?" This is all I heard every day, from my wake-up in the morning to bedtime at night. She would say how proud she would be if I were a priest and how all of her friends and relatives would be so happy if I were a priest. I kept telling her that I had no intention of entering the priesthood. This did not stop her constant nagging on the priest subject. My mother would ask me several times a week if any of the boys were interested in going into the priesthood–I said no. This bothered her, as I could see by the expression on her face.

As I said, this nun was all about screaming and hollering in the classroom, very little hitting or smacking the boys. Again, she only issued her wrath on the boys, never any of the girls. We were drilled on going to Confession on Saturday afternoon, and a reminder she would be taking roll at mass on Sunday. Halloween came and went with no fear anymore about the dead coming out of their graves to "haunt me." The Christmas candy routine repeated itself again. Here I was in sixth grade and never having enjoyed MY BOX of Christmas candy. I got a Jack Russell terrier and named her "Snoopy," after my favorite comic strip *Peanuts*. The dog lived until she was sixteen years old.

Springtime saw the initiation of school dances in the basement of the old school building. This was something that I had never experienced. Entrance to the dance on Saturday night was free and was chaperoned by several of the parents of the children. The dance included grades six, seven and eight. The boys stood on one side of the hall, the girls on the other side, not much interaction or dancing went on. I started to notice that a lot of the boys from my grade and other grades were much better dressed than me. I mentioned this to my mother, and she said, "You go to school to learn, not to be in a fashion show."

I owned one white dress shirt that I had to wear on Sunday to both the 9:00 a.m. children's mass and when I sang in the choir that same day. I would then try to wear the same shirt to school on Monday if I was able to keep it clean. The balance of the week I would wear a colored shirt, while the rest of the boys had white shirts on. My mother pissed and complained that she had to quickly wash the one white shirt for the next weekend's show. My mother could not iron a boy's/man's shirt to save her life! The collar would be iron flat like a women's blouse and the cuffs were always folded over. Finally, I asked her to buy a spray can of Niagara spray starch and I quickly learned how to iron my one white shirt. I asked my mother why I didn't have more than one white shirt, stylish boy's pants, and a sport coat that actually fit me. She replied, "I don't like buying you a lot of clothes, since you only get one season out of them." She had to buy me new shoes since you can't put this year's feet in last year's shoes!

The clothing wars continued for many years until I started to work part-time little jobs and bought my own clothes. We were NOT POOR. My father worked as a supervisor for the Philadelphia Water Department and was receiving a monthly retirement pension check from the Navy Department for his thirty years of military service. He had a new Mercury under his ass every four years and my mother had a collection of shoes and pocketbooks, enough to open a store. I guess it was called priorities. My mother constantly harped on me selecting to be a priest, to which I kept saying NO, but that was not what she wanted to hear. She also wanted to know how many of the girls would be going into the convent; I said that I didn't know that answer.

I graduated from sixth grade with passing grades. Ole Breatho did not hand out holy cards or intimidate my handwriting in front of the class. Looking forward to only two more years with the penguin herd.

My mother wanted to attend the Cannstatter Volkfest again this year. We dove there this time, and it didn't take as long since my father was more familiar with the location. The same routine: pay a fee and enter, picnic benches all over, German music, people with funny hats and wardrobes, and the smell of food. We sat at a picnic bench, and my father went to get a pitcher of beer and a bottle of Coke for me. My father had a glass of beer and said, "Let's go and get something to eat." My father got the knockwurst and sauerkraut sandwich, and I asked for and got the hot dog, sauerkraut, and mustard on the hot dog bun–what a treat! My mother seeing me with the hot dog on bun again complained "why did you get that, how do you know if the hot dog is properly cooked"? I pretended not to hear her and ate and thoroughly enjoyed this rare treat.

I got up to go to the bathroom, and my mother said, as she had instructed me many times before, "Do not use the soap in the bathroom, there are germs on it."

My father, either hearing her say this the first time (he had poor hearing, as his ears were damaged during the war when depth charges were dropped on his submarine), or had ignored her before said "Irene the boy will use the soap to wash his hands."

My mother tried to chirp in, "There are germs on soap in bathrooms."

Before she could continue, my father blasted out, "What do you think surgeons use to wash their hands before they operate?" An aura of silence fell upon the picnic table where we were sitting. There were other children there, running around, hollering, just having a good time. I said that I wanted to join them, but my mother said, "No you will sit here with us, and listen to me, I'm your mother, you will do as I say." But this time she had had more than a few beers in her and was slurring her words.

When she got up to go to the ladies' room, she was swaying and stumbling on her feet. I could always tell when my mother was lit up. She would have this goofy look on her face, slur her words, and stumble when she walked, and such was the case on this day. We stayed until it started to get dark and drove home. On the drive home, my mother, who was in the bag, had the balls to say, "Don't have any kids, it's not worth it." I ignored this remark from my drunken mother, but it still bothers me today to think my own mother sank to such a low spot in her life. My father had to help my mother upstairs to bed. I got a bath and went to bed, as tomorrow was the first day of school.

September 1961

Seventh Grade, Age Twelve

Same old, same old meeting in the schoolyard, seeing old friends, and telling stories about our summertime vacations. The old nun rang the school bell and yelled out the same BS "Silence, get in line, no talking, put the sign of the cross on your lips." Line up eighth grade here, seventh grade there, and so on. Again we were marched to the new school building to our classrooms. We sat in alphabetical order and saw our nun for this year.

This one was young, not your typical old snarly penguin. Since she was new, we had no prior knowledge of who she was or how she would handle us. We had the usual curriculum: religion twice a day, arithmetic, spelling, history, geography, English, writing a short story, and more of the stupid poetry. We also continued with verb conjugation and diagraming a sentence, for what reason I do not know.

Halloween, Christmas, and Easter all came at the appointed calendar times, all with the same flamboyance and usual letdowns as in previous years. In early spring, Mother Superior came to each of the seventh grade classrooms and ordered the girls out of the classrooms. The girls were absent from the classrooms for what seemed to be an hour. When they returned, they all acted very differently toward the boys. The boys all assumed that the nuns discussed the "ways of the world" with the girls and told the girls that "all boys are little pigs dressed up in boy costumes, stay away from them." At the spring dance, the girls avoided the boys as if we had the plague. The girls all stayed on one side of the gym floor and made no attempt to intermingle with the boys. This continued until the school year ended.

The young nun that we had in the classroom raised her voice probably no more than ten times during the entire school year. She did carry a wooden ruler in her pocket and would strike a boy's desk when she walked by. As usual, this nun did not show any anger toward the girls, all as part of their training at the convent. The Mother House probably directed all of the nuns to steer all of their anger and hate toward the boys only. My mother tried the "pizza giveaway" again, dragging me to the back door of the convent and introducing herself with "I'm Richard Etherton's mother." She continued to exchange pleasantries with the Sister, as she called her, and spilled out her life story with the nun. I had to stand there like the little asshole that I was and watch the shit show unfold. Hopefully this BS will not spill over to high school.

My mother continued to ask, "How many boys are going to become a priest?" I responded that only two boys talked about it, but were not committed. My mother continued to bagger me at least twice a week: "Why don't you become a priest, it would be so wonderful," and my response was NO. I started to believe in myself this school year, realizing that I was not the idiot in this story. I could see my mother as she really was, a very conniving, hateful, and spiteful person. My mother was happy only when she was arguing with someone. The beer drinking and smoking continued unabated, and yes, I had to accompany my mother and father on their jaunts to beer joints, clubs, etc., just to sit there and ask myself, "Why?"

One night, when my mother was lit up, she started to tell me about a boy who lived across Earp Street when she was growing up in South Philly. She said this boy's name was Jimmy, a sweet boy who always wanted to help her mother (my grandmother). My mother went on and on with a completely disjointed story. She stopped several times in the dissertation to say, "Why can't you be like Jimmy Kane, he was so thoughtful and kind." She went on and on for more than an hour, and this really bothered me, as my own mother was comparing me to some boy in her past. I really didn't care about what she was saying, but this was very disheartening to me.

I remember going to the barber shop before school started. The barber told me that I should trim my "unibrow." I asked him what that was, and he said, "When your eyebrow extends from one side to the other over the bridge of your nose." He said, "You can get tweezers and pull out the unwanted hairs. I thanked him for the information and went home after my haircut was finished. I told my mother that the barber said I had a unibrow and I should remove it with tweezers. My mother said, "Don't you dare, you can hurt your eyes." I went to my room, got tweezers, looked in the mirror, and started to pull out all of the unwanted hairs. I thought that I looked a lot better now. When my mother saw me, she exclaimed, "Why did you disobey me?" I just walked away and went outside.

I graduated from seventh grade, nothing exceptional, knowing that I had only one more year of penguin flu infestation.

September 1962

Eighth Grade, Age Thirteen

I made it to the last year of penguin BS! Again the school year started the same as in previous years. The old nun rang the school bell and barked out her usual orders, "Silence, no talking, put the sign of the cross on your lips," blah, blah, blah, "Eighth grade line up here," and so on.

Our last year was spent in the old school building, which now seemed like a dungeon. We marched up to our classrooms, "No talking, silence, put the sign of the cross on your lips," and we sat in alphabetical order again. I saw some new faces in the class, probably families moving into the parish. The eighth grade nun was short, old, and round, looking like some type of dwarf from a child's fairytale book. She lost no time in laying out her ground rules for the school year: "You are eighth graders, in your last year here at Hoy Child School, there will be no talking in this classroom, religion will be the most important subject that you learn this year, I will not hesitate to smack anyone who gets out of line," and "This year is pivotal for your future plans." OK, let's play ball, said the batter to the penguin umpire.

The curriculum was somewhat repetitive of the years gone by except we would be introduced to algebra as preparation for high school. I muddled through the year as best as I could, knowing this was the last time that I would have to listen to frustrated old women posing as teaching experts. As for the choir experience, I was now selected to lead the boy's choir group from the altar halfway down the main church aisle on when to stop and begin singing. Apparently, my voice in eighth grade was decent, as I was selected for a solo in the main church aisle. My mother and father would usually attend the 11:00 a.m. High Mass that the choir sang at. After mass she was simply ecstatic saying, "This is a sign from God, you must be a priest now." My standard response was NO.

She continued to hound me every day about entering the priesthood, as the seminary was selecting candidates when they graduated from the eighth grade. There was one boy, Patrick was his name, who planned to enter the seminary at the start of the freshman high school year. My mother, upon hearing this, exclaimed, "Why can't this be you? What a wonderful life Patrick has chosen." I was learning how to ignore her but still appear to be interested in what she had to say.

The eighth grade nun, who had no nickname, was a real taskmaster. She would assign homework every night that would take three to four hours to complete, and five to seven hours on the weekends. Her instructions were that "When you go home, do not watch that show "bandwagon" as you will be wasting your time, pay more attention to your schoolwork." She was referring to "Bandstand, which at the time was a local Philly afternoon dance show featuring high school kids dancing and having fun. She would say, "Suck on some hard candy when doing your assignments at home, it will keep you focused on your work." OK, how about tooth cavities and juvenile diabetes, you old turd!

Halloween, Christmas, and the Easter Holidays all followed their places on the calendar. With my knowing that this was the absolute last year that I would spend my Sundays and Holydays singing in a choir, having to get up at 4:30 a.m. on Christmas and Easter, and still attending the 9:00 a.m. children's mass every Sunday along with the choir attendance at the 11:00 a.m. High Mass, I felt relieved! I still had to give my box of Christmas candy to my mother, since this was the last year that I would have to go through the BS of the Christmas candy to my mother. Eight years in school, and I never enjoyed my Christmas candy.

The spring dance was different this year, as we all knew that we would probably not be seeing all of the crowd next year in the high schools that we were attending. Some of the boys were accepted to LaSalle High School, some even will be going to ST. Joseph Prep. I applied to LaSalle but failed the entrance exam. My mother could not believe this or accept the results. All of the kids in our eighth grade class graduated to high school. They took a graduation picture of our class. I would be attending Cardinal Dougherty High School, at 2nd and Godfrey Avenues in Philadelphia.

My mother has a small graduation party at our house on 15th Street. My Aunt Ann and Uncle Bud were there with their two children. This was not a big exposé but just a small family get together, with my mother cooking dinner. It was a Saturday evening, and I was with three of my close friends who I went through grade school with. We all stopped by my house to see what was going on when my mother told me that she was having this small family gathering in honor of my graduation. I greeted my uncle and aunt and my cousins, and I said I would be going with my friends over to their house as there would be a small gathering of the kids from school, and I would be home soon. We would probably listen to records and maybe dance a little. My mother immediately said, "You are not going anywhere, you will stay here with us" and "I am your mother, and you will listen to me." She told my friends to leave as I would be staying there. A bitter woman even at my grade school graduation. The night at home dragged out as a unmerciful punishment for a crime yet to be determined. To quote Stalin: "Find me a crime and I will find you a man guilty of it." The drinking and smoking all continued and sickened me.

I can truthfully state that during the eight years at Holy Child Parish School, I never saw the nuns hit, push, or smack any of the girls in the classrooms. These women, the nuns, who were charged with the education of younger children all took their frustrations out on the boys. These were women who were hell-bent on destroying the morale of boys and didn't care how they accomplished this task. My mother and father firmly believed that the priests and nuns could do no harm. They would be astonished today to learn of the allegations of the priests molesting young children. If I had been molested when in school, my parents would not have believed a word that I said. Thank GOD that I was one of the lucky boys who escaped this trauma.

*　*　*

In 2019 there was a small reunion of all the graduation classes of Holy Child School in the school auditorium. This was a chance to see some old familiar faces and share some laughs. There was food and drinks for all to enjoy there. I attended this function with my wife, Connie, but she did not attend the school or was a member of the parish. A woman approached me during the evening and said, "Are you Rich Etherton?,"

I responded, "Yes I am."

She began the conversation with saying, "I remember your mother," and this caught my immediate attention. She continued: "Your mother was walking with you on Broad Street, probably walking you back to school since it was lunch time. We were only in fourth grade and it was when we had to return our signed report cards back to school, your mother approached me and said, 'I'm Richards mother, are you in his classroom?' I responded that yes I was. Your mother demanded that I show her my report card, and, being intimidated by this overbearing woman, I showed her my report card. Your mother said that my grades were not as good as Richard's, and handed back my report card. The interaction with this person left me trembling and uneasy to say the least. I remember that day as if it happened just yesterday."

I apologized for the rude actions of my mother and explained that this was her method of operation with everyone.

That summer my mother took me to get working papers as I had a part-time job lined up at the Logan Paint and Hardware Co. on Broad Street. I would be hired as a stock boy, filling the empty shelves in the store and putting away the deliveries that came in. It was also a great opportunity for me to learn the names of various tools, screws, fasteners, types of paint, how-to cut-glass panes, and eventually cut keys. The price of new keys at this time was two keys for twenty-five cents.

Also that summer, a letter from Cardinal Dougherty High School arrived, explaining the basic rules and regulations for the upcoming high school year. The most important was the dress code: no long hair, hair to be kept short and trimmed, shined dress shoes, sport coats, and ties at all times, clean-shaven, lunch can be brought to school but is also for sale in the cafeteria, and various day-to-day. My mother saw this and started to complain about the dress code. "We will have to go out and get sport coats and shirts and ties. I hate to buy you clothes for you as you only get one season out of them."

The next Saturday my father drove us down to South Street. We went into a USED MEN'S clothing store. My mother picked out two used sport coats, which were the style for a man in his fifties, not for a young boy of fourteen. I didn't even get to select the color of the coats. My mother wrote a check for the two sport coats, and we left the store and drove to the Sears store on Roosevelt Boulevard. I hated these two coats with all of my being. We were not poor; why did I have to wear a used sport coat from someone that I never knew or wanted to know? My mother purchased two white shirts and two ties at the Sears store, along with two pairs of trousers. The sad fact is that my mother did not take these two used sport coats to the dry cleaners. Both coats had stains on them which I had to live with. So, I had two white shirts added to the one that I already had, which I wore for the five-day week, washed them, and ironed them using my spray can of Niagara starch. Such was my shitty ass wardrobe for my first year in high school. I worked at my part-time job during the summer and looked forward to high school with no BS.

October 1962, the Cuban missile crisis. The world stood still as President Kennedy challenged Nikita Khrushchev, the Russian premier, on the placement of Russian missiles in Cuba, ninety miles away from Florida and the U.S. mainland. We were at the brink of nuclear World War III at that point in time. It wasn't disclosed until fifty years later that the Russian submarines near the east coast of the United States at that time were armed with nuclear-tipped torpedoes. It was at this time I started to become interested in world events and politics in general.

Photo Album

My mother when she graduated from West Phila Catholic Girls H.S.

4817 N. 15 Street circa 1947, my father's Plymouth in driveway

4817 N. 15 Street, Philadelphia circa 1960 with mom & dad

Riding a mechanical horse on the boardwalk with dad watching

PHOTO ALBUM 51

My uncle Frank, me, and my aunt Betty on the beach in Atlantic City N.J.

The author and his mother outside our house on Georgia Ave, Atlantic City N.J.

The author and childhood friend in our 1950 winter style clothing

Father, mother, and me, 1954 in my aunt's kitchen, Norfolk Virginia

My dog Snoopy

Mom and I outside our house on Georgia Ave Atlantic City N.J.

Cub Scout picture 4th or 5th grade

Confirmation suit, which just fit me from previous year's Communion; the little girl was the daughter of mom's acquaintance

5th or 6th grade school picture

The second floor of the building at Carlisle St. and Fishers Ave. used as an improvised school room during five years

Four improvised rooms (with plastic partitions open)
in auditorium of the old school building

FATHER KELLY WITH CHOIR BOYS AND MEN'S CHOIR

Circa 1958, men and boys choir, author is to the right and circled

Residence at Carlisle St. and Fishers Ave. Used for five years for school purposes, before the erection of the new annex

High School Graduation, June 1967, with my mother and father

Holy Child parish and school 5200 N. Broad St.
As a perspective, the Broad Street Run goes directly past the location

4817 N. 15 Street, Philadelphia. circa March 2023, abandoned and boarded up

September 1963

Age Fourteen, Freshman Year of High School at Cardinal Dougherty

To get to school, I would walk from my house up to Broad Street about three blocks away. I would cross Broad Street and go down the steps to the subway platform, where I would take the subway north to the end of the line at the Fern Rock Station. There, I would go up the stairs and take the XO route bus, which would drop me off in front of Cardinal Dougherty High School. The first day was delegated to the freshman class only. We were directed into the auditorium, where we sat awaiting names and assigned classrooms. The atmosphere was quite different, as the school was entirely staffed by either priests, brothers, or lay teachers, NO PENGUINS! NO OLD NUN RINGING A SCHOOL BELL NO HOLLERING, "SILENCE PUT THE SIGN OF THE CROSS ON YOUR LIPS!"

Names were called out and you were assigned to "sections." I was assigned to Section D11. The letter D signified Freshman classman. C was for sophomores, B was for the junior class, and A designated the senior classman. The freshmen all moved to their designated homerooms, where we met our homeroom teacher, a priest. We were seated in alphabetical order and handed our "rosters," or class schedules, along with a key to our designated locker. There were a lot of rules and regulations such as: don't lose your locker key, make sure you have the correct book for the class that you are attending, there are certain upstairs and downstairs in the building (which had three floors), don't be late in the mornings or late for your classes. You ate lunch in the cafeteria in the basement area, and there was also a school store to purchase notebooks, gym clothes, etc. The first week of high school was a real eye-opener. The curriculum consisted of religion, geometry, English, world history, Latin, mechanical drawing, and gym. NO DAMN POETRY!

I looked around at the other boys, who all had decent sport coats on, and here am I with a used coat that looked like I had borrowed it from a great old uncle. Well at least I had new shoes, since you can't put this year's feet in last year's old shoes.

Our first scheduled test was in world history, and I got a mid-80s test result, which shocked me. The next day, there was a selection for the Student Council for the freshman class, and I was selected. So I was handed a bright white badge that I had to wear on my sport coat at all times. When I came home and told my mother that I was selected to the Student Council, she said, "This is a wonderful thing, GOD is with you." Mid-September, the school announced that there would be a parent meeting at the school one evening during the week. The meeting was to introduce the school and teaching staff to the parents. I told my mother so she could plan on attending. My mother said, "You will go with me on that night," I responded that it was for parents only. My mother said in her usual demanding tone of voice "I'm your mother and you will do what I tell you to."

So, the appointed night came, and my father drove me and my mother to the high school. I still had on my clothing attire with my Student Council button on, from that school day. We entered the school through the front main doors, and guess who the first priest was who saw me? Father Peck, the high school disciplinarian. This man was very intimidating; he would drag you out of line in a heartbeat and berate you for his own personal fun. He was the priest that you were sent to when you got in any type of trouble during the school day. Father Peck immediately asked me, "Why are you here, what type of trouble have you caused?"

I responded, "This is my mother, and she wanted me to accompany her tonight, and I'm not in any trouble."

My mother introduced herself and went with her usual rambling of "I graduated from West Catholic Girls High School, I grew up in South Philly, I attended The King of Peace Catholic Church blah, blah, blah." Father Peck said that this school meeting was for the parents, and not the students. My mother said that she wanted me to accompany her as she met my teachers." Father Peck exchanged pleasantries with her, and we moved along to the next stop, the homeroom and religion priest. We met the homeroom priest and he immediately asked, "Why are you here?" I explained that my mother wanted me to accompany her. So my mother went into her rehearsed speech, graduate of West Catholic Girls High school, grew up on Earp Street in South Philly, attended Christ The King of Peace Catholic Church, blah, blah, blah. This little off-Broadway skit went on all night as we went from classroom to classroom. Thank GOD there were no other student there to exploit my embarrassment in class the next day.

I asked my mother why she went out of her way to humiliate me, and she said it was because she wanted the priests and professors (she called the lay teachers "professors," which they were not), to know that she was my mother. So goes my motherly interventions in my first year in high school. We met the athletics teacher, she introduced herself with the same line of BS blah, blah, blah. She told this gentleman that she didn't want me to take any aggressive gym classes because of my heart." WHAT, I never had a bad heart, nor do I have a bad heart today!

The gym teacher told my mother to "get a cardiologist note stating my condition." Nothing happened with getting a note. I asked my mother why she said this, and she said gym was not really important in school, "I don't want you to hurt your heart." What a line of BS, I took the gym class and "didn't hurt my heart," as my mother predicted; I just wish that she had stayed out of my life at that time of my development.

As I previously stated, lunch was in the cafeteria. My mother made my lunch and had it ready for me when I came down for breakfast every morning. I would tell her what I wanted for lunch, but she made the sandwich the way she wanted to. Every damn sandwich was made on white bread with butter, even on meatless Fridays, cheese on white bread and no mustard. I hated a lot of the lunch meats that she used on the sandwiches and told her what I liked and what I disliked. My comments made no difference, as she would say, "You will eat what I give you and like it." At lunch, we sat at long tables with swivel seats. I noticed that a lot of the boys would trade their sandwiches with each other. I asked one of the guys sitting next to me if he wanted to trade sandwiches. He looked at what I had and said "No, you eat fucked up food." I remember his exact words spoken then. None of the other boys ever wanted to trade sandwiches. The cafeteria would have a weekly fixed menu at lunch time. There would be pizza, hoagies (submarine sandwiches), mashed potatoes with beef gravy, and a host of other foods. The smell of the hoagies being prepared would waft up the stairways and into the corridors, and my appetite would go off the chart. I told my mother that I wanted to buy a hoagie on the designated day for my lunch, and not take her sandwich. Her response was "No, you will eat what I give you and like it," or "how do you know that the sandwiches are fresh, and what type of lunch meat is being used?" I was not able to buy my lunch during my freshman year at high school.

November 22nd, 1963, President John F. Kennedy was assassinated in Dallas Texas. I heard about the shooting on the way home from school that day. Everything in this country came to a complete halt on that day. We only had four television stations back then, no cable in any home at that time, and all of the stations were line-to-line with the coverage of the assassination of the president. School was closed for three days, as well as many places of business. This was a defining day in the history of this country. Vice President Lyndon Johnson became president, and the Vietnam War was in full swing. There were daily reports on the news of American soldiers who were killed in action.

After the Christmas break, I saw Patrick at Cardinal Dougherty one day. I asked him why he was here, and he said the priesthood was not for him. I told my mother that Patrick was no longer studying at the seminary and that he gave up on the priesthood. My mother was devastated when hearing the news, as she could not understand why. This bothered her for weeks, as she continually brought up the topic of Patrick. I graduated from my freshman year to my second year at Cardinal Dougherty High School. I continued to work at my part-time jobs earning and saving some money. I also started to "caddie" at two local golf courses: Ashbourne and Melrose. My father would drive me to the golf course and drop me off on a Saturday morning. After learning the ropes of being a caddie, I would carry two golf bags for eighteen holes and get paid ten dollars, a big payday for me.

My first summer away from grade school turned out to be ok. I used some of my earnings to buy some decent shirts and ties for school. The guys went downtown to the Shirt and Tie Corner. Good quality shirts and ties at extremely reasonable prices. I continued my Niagara spray starch and ironing routine on my new shirts. At least I had some new shirts and ties to wear to school next semester. I also had some money from my part-time jobs, so I went to Lit Brothers Department Store (an old-time department store in Philly at 8th and Markets Streets), and I was able to buy a navy-blue sport coat! WOW, my own, new sport coat that I bought with my money, not my parents'. Now I did not have to wear the used sport coats that my mother purchased for me, what a relief.

The smoking and drinking continued, but my mother was slowly moving away from beer. Her new liquid refreshment was Christian Brothers Port Wine. She purchased this in a half gallon bottle at the Officers Club at the Philadelphia Navy Yard at a ridiculous low price. Times were a-changing.

September 1964

Second Year at High School, Age Fifteen

I moved up to Section B-5, since I had decent test scores from the first year. The curriculum that year was religion, Algebra I, world history, mechanical drawing, Spanish 1, gym, and biology. I did not seek a return to the Student Council position. I saw Patrick almost every day, and always said hello to him. I would mention to my mother that I spoke to Patrick, and she would say, "Why isn't he at the seminary studying for the priesthood?" She just can't admit that the priesthood is a special calling, and not everyone answers that call.

I had a biology class with a priest named Father Foster, a large, imposing man. He carried dice in his pocket and a large wooden paddle tied to his waist. If he caught you screwing around in class, he called you up to the front of the classroom. The practice was that he would roll the dice, you would then roll the dice and must beat his roll. If he won, the difference between his roll and your roll was the number of paddles that you would get. You would bend over and hold your ankles, and he used two hands to hold the paddle to whack your ass! If your dice roll beat his, it didn't matter; you would roll again until he won. Father Foster never lost at this game.

There weren't any earth-shattering occurrences that year and I graduated with good grades and moved on to my junior year at Cardinal Dougherty High School. I still worked the summer at part-time jobs and at the golf courses as much as possible. The Vietnam War was the main topic in the news every day, and the draft was becoming a reality for more and more younger men.

February 16th, 1965, I turned sixteen and went for my driver's license, I flunked the verbal test the first time but passed the second time around. My father bought a 1953 Plymouth from a neighbor on the street, for a price of sixty-five dollars. This car was a real junker: the front seat was ripped with the springs showing, the floor on the driver's side was rotted away, the opening was covered with several floor mats, the car had a heater that hardly worked. There was no radio, the transmission was a standard three-speed on the steering column (three on the tree, as it was called), the headliner was ripped and hung down in the rear seat area, and you had to coax the car to start– but it was a means of transportation!

My father and I went to a junkyard to find a replacement front seat. We measured the width of the existing front seat and the bolt pattern in the floor. After removing the seat in Plymouth, we found that the seat from a 1958 Ford would fit in the car, but only the front seat bolts would line up with those of the Plymouth. We took the seat out of the Ford and installed it in the Plymouth, with only the front set of bolts holding the seat in the Plymouth. We left the old Plymouth's ripped seat at the junkyard and drove home. God help me if I was in a frontal crash: since the seat was not bolted in the rear location, the entire seat would have cantilevered forward and pinned me into the steering wheel, and the front seat passenger would have sailed through the windshield.

Remember this was 1965 and seatbelts were a novel item, even in new cars. So I learned to drive a manual transmission and operate the clutch and gas pedal at the same time. My father was able to get for me a piece of sheet metal that would fit over the opening in the floor on the driver's side. I cut the sheet metal to fit as best as I could, and installed the sheet metal over a coating of roofing tar that came in a gallon can. The sheet metal also had several sheet metal screws applied. I had to cut a round hole in the new floor, as the master brake cylinder was located under the floor on the driver's side. The master cylinder occasionally leaked, so I bought a can of brake fluid and filled the master cylinder when the brake pedal felt soft and squishy. My friend Mike and I decided to paint the car, as the original color was a faded blue. My father was able to get a five gallon can of "battleship gray" from the Navy Yard. My best friend Mike and I washed the car and filled in any surface rust spots with a product called "Bondo," made for automobile body repairs. We used a brush to cut in the close spots and then used a standard paint roller and painted the entire car "battleship gray." The '53 Plymouth looked great. We also painted the wheels a combination white-and-black triangle.

I now had my own personal transportation to and from high school. I went to a car radio shop and was able to purchase a used but functioning car radio, AM only in those days. I installed the radio and it worked, and I made a wooden faceplate to cover the huge opening in the front of the dash and surround the radio–it looked great. One of the major problems with this old car was the fact that the engine would run hot in the summer months. I had to constantly check the coolant level in the radiator at least three times a week and add new coolant. The oil pressure was low, so back in those days, you would add a can of STP to the oil, which would help to keep the oil pressure up. For all of the problems, this was my first car and got me around town and on my first big date.

That summer I met the girl of my dreams on a park bench in our neighborhood. Her name was Connie, and I told my friend Mike that someday I would marry her. After a rocky start, we began to date, and I took her out in my Plymouth. She was either amazed or overcome with fear as she sat in this recreated car. A good start on the first date: a spider came down from the headliner and scared the shit out of her. This was just the beginning. When I told my mother that I was dating a girl in the neighborhood, the sixty questions began: are they Catholic, do they go to church, what is her mother's name, what is her father's name, what nationality are they, where does the father work, was he in the military service, where did they live before they moved here, blah, blah, blah– typical for my mother's advances into everyone that she met. Finally Connie's father accepted me (somewhat), and I was able to sit with her in their living room after a short date.

One such time while I was with Connie at her house on a Saturday night, the doorbell rang, and my mother and father were both at the front door. They were invited in and began talking with Connie's mother and father; I knew this was not a good scene. They stayed for about twenty minutes and left. My mother had had a few drinks in her, as she was stumbling over her words and swaying in the house. I do remember hearing my mother repeat her life story: South Philly, graduate of high school, blah, blah, blah. I also heard her ask Connie's father where he worked and if it was a steady job. My mother had no filter with any subject with any person—she just let it spew out. When I got home that night, my mother started, "Don't get involved with them, the mother sits by herself watching television, and the father sits in the dark listening to music," and "They come from a poor neighborhood, don't get involved." I ignored her and I went to bed.

That summer I signed up for a summer school class in advanced algebra that was given at the Northeast High School at Cottman and Algon Streets in Northeast Philadelphia. The class was given in the morning, and I was home by 12:00 p.m. I was able to continue at my part-time jobs all summer. One time during the summer school algebra session, my father told me to take his 1964 Mercury to school that day. What a bad move that was. I parked his car right outside the classroom in a safe area with other cars. When I came out after class my heart stopped beating. The Mercury had extra cost fancy wheel covers, which were now gone, stolen! I did not want to take the drive home, knowing the hollering that I would be subjected to. When I got home, I told my mother about the stolen wheel covers. She started to rant and rage, "Why did you allow the wheel covers to be stolen, why did you park there?" and "Wait until your father comes home."

I spent the afternoon projecting the additional screaming and hollering when my father came home. My father came through the front door and the shit show started. My mother started to scream and tell my father that the wheel covers were stolen off his Mercury. Then my father started yelling and hollering, "Why did you let the wheel covers be stolen, why didn't you park in a safe area? After supper we will drive up to the school to see where the car was parked."

I responded, "Looking where the car was parked will not bring back the wheel covers." We drove to the Northeast High School, and I asked my friend to go with me on this venture into hell. We parked where the car was earlier in the day, and my father got out of the car and walked around, looking in the grassy areas. Did he think the wheel covers were there? We got back in the car and drove home, and all the time my father was ranting about why I let the wheel covers be stolen. My friend in the back seat said, "It's not like there was a sign on the car that said, 'please steal the wheel covers.'" There was silence until we got home, and then my mother added into the jibber jabber. That was the last time that I took my father's car to school. I continued to work at my part-time jobs, and I saved enough money to buy all of the clothes that I needed for school in the fall semester. I would never again rely on my parents to buy for me any piece of clothing, as I could even afford to buy my own shoes.

September 1965

Third Year at High School, Age Sixteen

I was in section B-5. I had been dating Connie over the summer and I was falling in love with her; she was special to me. Classroom subjects this year were about the same as the previous year, with Spanish II, algebra and trigonometry, mechanical drawing, English/short story writing (no damn sentence diagraming), history, and, of course, religion. I took the PSAT test this year and I remember that I scored above average but can't remember the exact score. There was a lot of talk among the guys as to where they thought they would go to college. My mother still asked if any of the boys were going into the priesthood. My response was an emphatic NO.

Cardinal Dougherty held student dances in the gym on special occasions and holidays. I always asked Connie to go with me and we had a great time dancing and talking to my friends. I was so proud to have Connie by my side and always wanted to show her off to the other guys. Our relationship grew and grew. I remember celebrating Christmas and buying her some small presents that I wrapped in gala holiday paper. Here I was taking my time and putting in effort to wrap a present for someone that I loved, what a feeling. It reminded me of all the previous Christmas times that my mother never had the time or ambition to wrap any of my Christmas presents. Priorities I guess were misplaced. The year went rather smoothly, looking forward to my senior year in high school. The Vietnam war raged on, with body counts being presented every night on the national news. Some of the guys were talking about the draft and what other options were available. I graduated with decent marks to my senior year of high school.

September 1966

Fourth Year at High School, Age Seventeen

I was now in section A-4. The curriculum was about the same: religion, advanced math with calculus, current world events, English, Spanish. I continued to date Connie and my love for her grew with time. We attended every school dance at Cardinal Dougherty and my senior prom. I took the college boards and scored 1188 total out of 1600. The school said that this was a good score. I applied to both Drexel Institute of Technology and Temple University and received acceptance letters from both schools. I applied for financial assistance but was declined, as my father was making a decent salary from the City of Philadelphia and he was receiving a Government Pension for being in the Navy for thirty years. The letter stated that our family was in a "middle income bracket, and financial aid was not warranted at this time." Since money was the principle object and not available at home, I had to plan otherwise for my future.

I graduated from Cardinal Dougherty High School with decent grades, being in the top 10% of the graduating class, thus ending twelve years of Catholic schooling. I looked into apprenticeship programs in the city-wide area. I took the apprentice test and scored a 92 out of 100 questions. I selected to apply at the Budd Company in Philadelphia and was accepted for an apprenticeship as a Toolmaker. The Budd Company manufactured automotive body stampings for the Detroit automakers. I started my apprenticeship the week after high school graduation. I elected to attend night school at Drexel, which at the time would be paid for by the Budd

Company providing that you carried at least a grade 80. My mother and father were relieved, since they didn't have to pay for any college education.

I worked at my apprenticeship at the Budd Company and continued with night school at Drexel. Connie and I were engaged, and I purchased a decent-sized engagement ring. Connie and my mother did not get along at all. There was always an aura of friction in the air when they were together. My mother made a remake to Connie saying, "I hope that you enjoy that ring, since it is not paid for." I paid for this ring in full, with my money that I was earning. Why my mother would say such a thing was extremely irritating. This remark was another example of my mother's inward hate and cynicism. My mother never offered congratulations to me and Connie on our engagement.

Connie and I were married on November 15th, 1969, at her church. We honeymooned at Cove Haven in the Pennsylvania Pocono mountains. Connie paid for the reception, which was at the Liberty Ballroom, and I paid for the honeymoon. We were both the only child in each family and had to pay for our wedding festivities. We lived in a small but new apartment off Fishers Avenue in the Olney section of North Philadelphia. We had one car, which Connie used daily to go to work, and I rode the streetcar and bus to work at the Budd Company. We were happy in our own private world. I completed my apprenticeship and took a job as a Junior Mechanical Engineer with a company in Springtown, PA, and continued with pursuing an engineering degree from Drexel. Connie was working with a company in Doylestown, PA.

I elected to join the Naval Reserves, Aviation, and spent a combination of both active and reserve time. When I was away, Connie received a bill from Sears for payments on our kitchen set. This was the "wedding gift" from my mother and father. Connie called my mother and asked what this bill was for, as we both were told the kitchen set was a gift. My mother said that "she didn't want to pay for it anymore," so we paid for our so-called gift. We also moved into our house in Churchville, PA.

My mother and father moved from 15th Street in Philadelphia to be with my mother's close relatives in Chesapeake, Virginia.

* * *

I will move forward in the story to 1972. I applied for and was accepted to an engineering job with a precision grinding company in Northeast Philadelphia. I received a phone call at home one evening from my aunt in Virginia. Apparently, my mother was drinking too much, tripped over their dog, fell, and broke her hip. She was in the Naval Hospital in Portsmouth, Virginia.

My aunt visited my mother in the hospital and said my mother was saying that if she had the opportunity, she would jump out the window at the hospital. My aunt told the hospital staff that they would carefully monitor her. I called my father and told him that I would make arrangements to fly to Virginia to visit my mother in the hospital. I made the trip and saw my mother in her hospital bed. She really didn't want me to be there. I spent two days at my mother's and father's house in Virginia, visiting my mother in the hospital, then returned home. Connie became pregnant with my daughter in 1973, and our world changed to a whole new chapter in our lives.

My beautiful daughter was born in 1974 and grew into a little ball of energy. We decided to fly to Virginia when my daughter was about the age of one. We stayed at a motel that was near my parents' house and my mother was pissed as she wanted us to stay with her. I explained to her that her house was small, and my daughter was not prone to "just sit down and be still," as she always said to me when I was growing up. I had a rental car, which I used to get us around to visit my aunt and cousins in Virginia. We ate breakfast at the motel, which set my mother off even further, as she wanted us to have every meal at her house. I had called her one morning that we were staying at the motel to tell her that we would be coming over later that day. My mother said, "Don't bother as me and your father are going out for the day." I know that they were not going anywhere that day. This was just one of her little shit moves that she thought would get me angry, but it didn't. I had privately asked my father where they went today, and he said, "No place, we were here all day."

We would have dinner with my mother and father, which turned into a real festival of nerves. My mother was constantly telling my little daughter, "Don't touch the dog, let the dog alone," and "Why aren't you eating what I put in front of you?" This started to irritate my wife, as I could see it in her facial expressions. We sat in the backyard of my parents' house one evening, and my mother said, "Thank God that we live far away so we don't have to babysit for you." My wife immediately shot back, "Don't worry, I would never ask you to babysit for my children." We flew back to our home in Churchville and continued our lives. But the weekly phone calls to my mother were exasperating on my part. I could immediately tell that she was in the bag by the way she slurred her words and didn't make any sense with her conversation.

I completed my Naval service in 1976 and was honorably discharged at the rank of AT1 (E6) Avionics, Patrol Plane Squadron, Senior Air Crew, flying many ASW patrols. 1977 saw the birth of my son and our first trip to Disney World later that year. Again my mother was pissed, as she couldn't understand why we didn't want to visit her in Virginia instead of going to Disney. We did drive to Virginia several times, as both of my children grew up, and we stayed in local motels as there was no extra room at my parents' house. Also, the screaming and hollering there was intolerable. As time passed, I dreaded the travel to my parents' house in Virginia, as a shit show would be in the making.

I had a job as an engineer with a precision grinding company in Philadelphia. There were a few times that I had to go on a business-related trip, usually to Chicago. I would casually mention my upcoming trip to my mother, saying that I would be away for a few days. She would go off the rails saying that someone should go with me on the trip, so as not travel alone. I would ignore her and change the subject.

1979 saw me form my own small business as an engineering and precision manufacturing company. My "at home time" was severely degraded, as I would be up late at night designing, preparing customer proposals, addressing customer issues, etc. My travel time would be consuming a tremendous amount of my time. I would always call my mother twice a day, as she requested, morning and in the evening. When I was working at home late at night, sometimes I would get caught up in my several work projects and forget to call her. The phone would ring late in the evening, and it was my mother asking why I hadn't called her. I would explain that I was working late, and her response was "Why do you do this? It is not necessary." I would listen to her ranting and say goodnight.

In 1981, my mother's brother in Virginia passed away from cancer. During my daily phone calls to her, she would start saying that she didn't want to live in Virginia anymore, she wanted to move back to PA. I would hear her complain to me every time we talked on the phone, even calling me when I was away on a business trip. She demanded that I start looking for a house for her and my father. My wife and I would contact realtors and then go out to see the offerings, but we looked for almost a month without any success. She became so intent on her quest, that she started to tell me, "If you don't find me a house, I will kill myself." This being her exact words. Of course she was drunk at the time of these calls, as she would constantly slur her words and tell me that I was not much of a son if I didn't find a house. I would hear the same threat each time I called her on the phone, wondering if I was bringing stress on me as I had a business to run and a wife and two small children to provide for. My mother demanded that the house have a garage and a fenced-in yard for the fleabag dog.

Eventually my wife and I found the house, a ranch-type in Bensalem, not far from her brother and his wife. I signed the offer agreement and made a deposit of five thousand dollars using my money. I made arrangements to fly to Virginia and then fly my mother up to inspect the house and sign the actual sales agreement with the realtor. She saw the house and said that it was great. She stayed overnight at our house, and my wife and daughter slept in our bed, my son was in his room, and my mother slept in my daughters room, I slept on the sofa in the living room. The next morning we flew back to Virginia, and as soon as we entered her house, my mother said to my father, "The place is alright but not as nice as we have here."

So much for turning around statements. I returned to the airport and found that the return flight to Philly was overbooked and there were no standby options on any other flights (this was Memorial Day weekend). My only option was to rent a car, pay the one-way rental fee and drive back to the Philly airport, pay the parking fee, and get my car out of the airport parking lot. I arrived at my home after 2:00 a.m. Saturday morning. My mother had called my house to see if I had arrived home and my wife told her that I had to drive home. So much for this enjoyable excursion.

The sale was finalized, and a settlement date was set, along with selling the house in Virginia. My wife and I spent a lot of time on the weekends at the Bensalem house cleaning, doing some minor repairs, painting, and trash removal. My mother would call at the house, and demand what we were doing there, as she said nothing had to be done to the house as she had inspected it. She was always in the bag when she called and would tell me to stop what we were doing there as she didn't want any changes made. Eventually these calls turned into her screaming in the phone at me for no apparent reason, and my wife began to get extremely mad at her BS.

The house in Virginia was sold, the settlement made, and movers scheduled to pack up the house and move northward. The movers specifically told my mother that NO flammable items could be loaded into the moving van. Of course my father ignored this and packed up his paints, thinners, etc. in cardboard boxes and covered the items with other belongings. There was a lawsuit brewing if the movers truck caught fire with his crap in the cardboard boxes. The relatives said goodbye to my mother and father and some tears were shed as we drove away (with me driving). As soon we got far enough away, my mother said, "Thank God I'm out of there." So much for putting on two faces with the relatives.

The move took place over the Labor Day weekend. I asked my wife to call various motels in the Bensalem area for a one-night room rental, as the moving van would not arrive at the new house until the next morning. My mother was pissed that she and my father and fleabag dog could not stay at our house overnight and would be forced into a motel room: "I'm your mother, why are you doing this to us?" I had no room for them at my house along with their flea-ridden dog, so they stayed at the motel for the one night. My father wanted me to put his crappy car in my garage overnight so no one would steal it; believe me no one would want that car!

The next morning I went to pick them up at the motel, and all I heard was ranting: "You left us alone in a strange place, how could you?" I drove to a local diner for breakfast, and I sat in the car with the fleabag while they went in to eat. They came out in less than ten minutes. I asked what the issue was, and her response was, "There is nothing in there that we want to eat, let's go to the house now."

We arrived at the house as the moving van pulled up in the driveway and began to unload the contents. As soon as the living room furniture was brought in, my father wanted me to hook up the TV to the antenna. I did so and he wanted to watch the Phillies, so he sat there while I worked with the movers on bringing in the furniture and setting up the bedrooms. My mother was in the kitchen with the pots and pans, complaining about every damn thing under the sun. As the day went on, I called my wife and asked her to get two Italian hoagies (submarine sandwiches) and bring them over for my mother and father for lunch, as there was no food in the house at this time. My wife and the sandwiches arrived, and I went home for a few hours and said that I would be back later that day. When I returned, the first thing my mother said was "We did not eat those sandwiches, just picked off some of the lunchmeats, this is not the kind of food that we like." OK, thank you also for being a pain in my ass at this time. The day ended with my mother having a couple glasses of her Christian Brothers Port Wine and stumbling around and mumbling her words. I said goodnight and went home.

The next day, I woke up early, checked on my messages and business dealings, and went over to the new house. The first thing was that my mother wanted to go to the local supermarket, the Acme being the closest. My father stayed home farting around in the garage, while I did the shopping with Mother at the Acme. We finished and returned to the house, and all the time my mother complained about everything that came into her mind. I finished up bringing in the groceries and then took her to the local bank to set up new accounts. I finished the day and went home with a splitting headache and resumed my business activities.

Within a month they had settled in, and my mother said they wanted to go to the Philadelphia Naval Hospital and the Navy Yard, and I was the one to show my father how to get there from Bensalem. So I planned my day to away from my responsibilities and drove them to the Naval facilities in South Philly. My father asked, "How can we get to Broad Street form Bensalem?" I responded that we will going down I 95 South, which is the easiest route. I also said that you avoid the traffic until after 9:00 a.m. during the week. We set out and as soon as we were on the 95, my father started, "You are going too fast, slow down." I responded that you have to move with the flow of the traffic and stay out of the far-left lane. He was notorious for driving below the speed limit and staying in the left lane, while the passing motorists threw glaring looks of hate at him.

We made it to our destination after constant screaming and hollering from the both of them. They went into the Naval Hospital to re-establish their residence here, and then to the Navy Yard. They wanted to go into the Navy Exchange (PX) and look around, then to the officers' club for beers and sandwiches for them. We left to return back to Bensalem and my father insisted that we drive up Broad Street and not on Interstate 95. We arrived back at their house, and I went home.

That Sunday I received a frantic phone call from my mother, saying that they were coming home from church and my father's car would not stop, so he pulled into the Exxon Gas station near their house. I had to go over and pick them up and drive them home. The next day my mother called me and said my father said that I had ruined his brakes because I was driving fast on 95. I said that I will never sit in or drive his car again.

The next Saturday (which was every Saturday) that I came over my father said that I was the cause of the brake failure. I just looked at him and ignored the statement. Ironically the next Saturday when I came over, he wanted me to leave my work early one day and change his spark plugs on the car. I said that I will have nothing to do with his car, and he should go to the gas station let them do it.

I would bring my children over on occasions and they would want to go in the yard and look around. One time my son and daughter picked some tulips from the garden and brought them in for my mother. My father hollered that they were ripping out the flowers. I said that we had to go home now and left. My mother wanted my children to come in the house and sit on the sofa, not touch the fleabag dog and just sit there. This did not bear well with me, so my children visited them only on rare occasions.

My Saturdays were spent at my parents' house in Bensalem. The routine was to arrive by 9:30 a.m., drive to the library to return or get new books, drive to the Super Fresh/A&P market because they had either Comet Cleanser for five cans for a dollar or canned string beans for four cans for a dollar, etc., then drive over to the Kmart to buy odds and ends that were on sale, drive back to the deli store for small quantities of lunch meats (dried beef being here favorite), then drive over to the Acme for food shopping. We would get in the check-out line and she would pay with a check. The cashier would call over the store manager to approve the check, and I watched the line grow longer behind my mother as her check was approved.

We would go to her house, and I would bring all of the items in and leave for my home around 1:30 p.m. Some weeks we would have to take the fleabag dog to the vets, since my mother said the dog was coughing a lot. The vet examined the dog and said nothing was wrong, then we drove back home to drop off the dog and start our routine. She refused to purchase stamps at the Acme at check-out time, saying "only the post office could sell stamps," so we drove to the post office and I stood in the line. There was a facility on Hulmeville Road as we drove back from the Kmart, the name being Livengrin. My mother asked what was in there, and I said the place is a detox center for alcoholics and druggies. My mother said, "I want to go in and look around."

I said, "Do you know anyone in there?" and she said no, just to look around. I quickly responded, "If you want to go and visit that place, call a cab to take you, as I have no intention of even taking you there." She got very pissy with me. One Saturday at the Acme, my mother wanted to get a piece of fresh fish. We walked back to the seafood area, and she started to ask the man behind the counter to see different types of fish. This went on for several minutes until she selected a specific fish, and had it weighed and wrapped, when she asked the price, she said, "Ohno, I don't want it now" and walked away from the seafood counter. I acted as I had no idea who this lady was. How can you go through the motions to purchase an item then upon hearing the price say that you don't want it?

She purchased a fruit cake for the Christian Brothers Monastery around Christmas. When I came over, she tried to persuade me to have a slice, I said no, as I absolutely hated fruitcake. I noticed that half of the fruitcake had been eaten. The next week when I came over, mother said we had to go to the post office, to return the fruitcake to the Christian Brothers Monastery. I asked why, and how much of the cake was being returned. She said, "I don't like the taste, and I'm sending half of the cake back." Are you kidding me, you ate half of the damn fruitcake and now you are returning the balance back for a full refund! She saw nothing wrong with what she was doing.

In 1985, I dissolved my Engineering Company due to business turndown and cash flow issues. I walked away owing nothing to any person or entity. All I heard from my mother was "I told you not to go into business, you had no idea as to what would happen, why put yourself through all of that aggravation, why don't you listen to me?" Thanks, Mom, for your faith in me. My wife and children all went on a little vacation to the Jersey shore, as the kids looked forward to this time away. My mother, as usual, complained as to why we were going away, but I ignored her.

In 1986, I applied for and was hired as an Engineering Supervisor with a local D.O.D. sub-contractor. I moved up to a General Supervisor Position, then finally to Principal Manufacturing Engineer, and spent thirty-four years there and retired in 2020. I had some travel time, and my mother, as usual, would complain as to why I had to go away and why was I alone and not with another person. Again, I ignored her.

My father passed away in 1989 at the age of 90. Every week before we went food shopping, we had to visit my fathers' grave at the cemetery. My mother suffered a minor heart attack and was hospitalized for a week. When she was released, she said that she needed at-home care. I said the hospital would provide a visiting nurse on a daily basis to check up on her and anything that she needed. This, coupled with her supplementary medical insurance coverage, would be completely covered. My mother said, "I will not have anyone coming into the house that I don't know" and "You should take me over to your house to care of me since I'm all alone." I responded that my house is all steps; what am I supposed to do, clear out a first-floor room and set up for your care? Also who is going to care for you during the day as my wife and I both worked? She responded, "You don't care for me at all since you won't take care of me." She would not allow the visiting nurse to come to the house, saying, "I will not allow any stranger in."

She stayed at her house, and I would stop by every day after my work day was finished. This went on for almost two weeks until I took her back to the cardiologist for a final exam and release from his care. She never let me forget that I didn't change my life around to care for her needs; I heard this tune constantly. My mother passed away in 1996 in the hospital after a short illness, and she is buried with my father.

Other Stuff and Sayings

Famous quotes from my mother:

–Boy are you a real dope.
–What a dumb bunny you are!

These were in reference to when I did something wrong. Certainly made a young boy feel great growing up.

–I am your mother, you will do what I tell you.
–Listen to what I tell you.
–You will obey me and don't ask why.
–Wait until your father comes home, he will deal with you.
–I will beat the living shit out of you.
–Sit down and be still, no moving around.
–Regardless of what you like, you will eat what I put on your plate
in front of you.
These threats were made almost on a daily basis as the mood hit her.

–They are nuts.
–There is something wrong with their heads.
–They belong in the nut house.
–Those people are crazy.
–Why would you want to bother with that stupid person.
–They are so drunk that they don't know what they are saying.
–They are retarded, don't bother with them.

—Don't get involved with Connie as her aunt is nuts and it probably runs in the family.

My mother said this to me after meeting Connie's aunt, who had a mild mental condition.

This was her standard method of describing anyone who didn't fit into her format of normalcy. Strange as it seems, a lot of it described her manners.

* * *

In the early sixties, my aunt adopted two children, both young girls. One of the girls had what was described as a "club foot." I remember being at my aunt's house and my mother harassing my aunt on why she adopted "such a child." I remember my aunt saying, that it was none of my mother's business, and to keep her comments to herself. We drove home to 15th Street and my mother talked about the child all the way home, to the point that it became disgusting for me to listen to as I sat in the back seat.

That weekend we drove out to visit my uncle in Bensalem, and my mother immediately started on the subject of the child with my aunt. My mother actually said to my aunt that my aunt should return the child to the orphanage since she had a club foot. This conversation went on for the entire time we were at my aunt's house. This is like getting a pet and then returning it to the store, what a sick and disgusting remark.

The following weekend, we were invited back to my aunt's/uncle's house in Bensalem for dinner on a Sunday. We sat down for dinner and my mother and father started to complain that were being served spaghetti and meatballs again. The mood around the dinner table became extremely cold. After dinner we were shown some pictures of my aunt's family and her mother who had lived in Italy before coming to this country. My mother, in her wisdom, made a comment about my aunt's mother, but I did not hear exactly what was said. Apparently, it was out of line, as my aunt said that we should go. We drove home and as soon as we entered our house, the phone rang. It was my aunt. I could hear her screaming at my mother through the phone. My mother started with her act and told my aunt, "Your mother looked old in the pictures, and her house looked like it was going to fall down." The next line was "I hate your guts and I wouldn't walk across the street to see you laid out in the funeral parlor." The phone was slammed down, and mother raved about this for the rest of the evening and into the next two days. The issue wasn't buried until just before my wedding.

Atlantic City

My mother and father bought a small (really small) row house in 1953 on Georgia Avenue on the block between Artic and Atlantic Avenues. The front porch was so small that I remember there was only room for two outdoor chairs. This house had two floors, consisting of a living room, large dining room, and a small kitchen. Upstairs there were two bedrooms and a small bathroom. There was no telephone in this house; if you wanted to make a phone call or have someone contact you, you had to use the phone at the corner store, called "Minnies." There was no television as my mother said it was not necessary. We also didn't have a radio, a basic necessity. There were no fans in this place, and I remember even as a small child it got stinking hot in there. I had to run the water in the kitchen and bathtub for a long period of time when I wanted a drink of water or to take a bath. The water would come out of the faucets in an orange color. My father said this was due to the old water pipes in the house.

My mother, grandmother, aunt, and myself would go to this house before Memorial Day and return to Philly just before Labor Day. My father would drive down and stay with us every Friday after work and drive back to Philly very early Monday morning. During the week I was a little boy growing up in a house with my mother and two older women in their seventies. The beach was only two blocks away from the house. My mother would take me to the beach once or, at the most, twice a week. We wouldn't stay at the beach very long, as my mother said she had to get back to take care of her mother and her sister.

Back at the house, I was NOT allowed to leave the porch area and play with the other kids on the same street–why, I do not know. My mother would take me to the amusements on the boardwalk once a week. The rest of the week at night was unbelievable for a small child. My mother, grandmother, and aunt would walk up Georgia avenue to the corner of Atlantic Avenue as darkness spread. There was a bar, (yes, a GOD damn bar) at the corner, called "Tina's." We would enter the place through the "ladies' entrance," which, back in those days, almost every bar had a side entrance for the ladies to enter rather than walk through the bar area. This entrance was down a long, partially-lit alley, and you would open the side door and you would be in the joint.

The place had an uneven wooden floor, which creaked when you walked on it. I have no idea how old this place was. There were old wooden tables with no tablecloths and hard wooden cane chairs. The tables were all arranged along a wall, and there was a "doorbell" attached to the wall at the end of the table. You would push the doorbell and the waitress would come from the bar area into this back room. My mother would order two pitchers of beer for the table and a small glass of Coke for me. My mother, grandmother, and her sister would all strike up their ciggies and fill the air with smoke as they drank their glasses of beer. I was allowed to get up from my extremely uncomfortable chair and just walk around the table. When my mother felt that I had had enough moving around, she would say, "Sit down and don't be moving around." I can actually remember my old bag of an aunt saying, "Irene, you should have him checked for worms since he can't sit still." So much for ever wanting to spend time around that woman.

I would get tired and sleepy, and I remember my mother saying, "Come on, we all have to leave now." She would order a quart of cold beer to take back to the house. We would then walk back to the little house and my mother would put me to bed on the pull-out sleeper sofa, where she and I would sleep. My mother and the other two would continue drinking their beer and smoking their ciggies in the dining room area. My grandmother and her sister would sleep in the bedrooms upstairs. The routine of walking up to Tina's, drinking beer, smoking ciggies, and bringing back a cold quart was a regular nightly occurrence. I can state this fact as the truth before GOD at any time! On the weekends my father would arrive, and some changes in the routine would occur. He would take me to the boardwalk amusements on both Friday and Saturday nights, as the cost of the tickets for the rides was extremely cheap. I remember some rides were as low as five cents. We would leave the boardwalk and, guess what, we would walk back to Tina's and, by now, my mother, grandmother and her sister had already staked their claim to a table in the back room. As I entered the room, those figures were partially obscured by the clouds of cigarette smoke. With my father there, I would now get two small glasses of Coke.

Usually on Saturday night, my father would say that he wanted to get steak sandwiches for supper. My father and I would walk down to the "White House" on Arctic Avenue to purchase steak sandwiches. What a place, the smells in there were different from anything that I had ever experienced. Steak sandwiches, hoagies (submarine sandwiches), French fries, peppers, onions, and all other types of food that I never knew existed. We would walk back to the bar with two steak sandwiches with lettuce and tomato. My father would cut them up for all at the table to enjoy, and I would get the smallest piece that could be presented. Never did we get fries with the sandwiches. We would eat the food and, of course, I would get fidgety as small kids do, and my mother would say, "Sit down stop acting up," or "no running around in here."

Eventually, as the evening wore on and the cigarette smoke started to burn my eyes, I would grow sleepy. My father would put two chairs together and I would lay down with my head on his lap and fall asleep. So here I was, a small child, asleep on chairs in a bar in Atlantic City, yet the beer consumption and cigarette smoking continued. I guess that my father carried me back to the house since I only remember waking up the next day on the sleeper sofa.

My father and mother would take me to the beach on Saturday afternoon for some period of time. When beach time was over, we walked back to the house, but would always stop at Tina's for a couple of beers first. The summer routine continued year after year until my mother sold the house, with some minor changes of dates to accommodate my school calendar. When my father was there on Saturdays, and Mom didn't want to go to the beach, we would drive down to Maynard's Bar in Margate. At the time, there were U.S. coins imbedded in the cement as you entered the bar from the street. There were silver dollars, half dollars, and quarters all in the cement, but the face sides of the coins were all visible. The same old routine: sit at a table, order beers and a small Coke for me, and tell me to sit still. I would watch men playing a game of shuffleboard and listen to them holler and curse. Eventually my father would take me outside and walk along the dock area where the big yachts were tied up. I would gaze at these large boats, wishing to be able to go on one of them to look around, but that never happened.

My mother sold the house in 1957 and made no profit, as she so stated.

* * *

I remember one summer, my aunt and uncle from Virginia traveled to visit and stay with us at the "house," which occurred only once. My aunt and uncle wanted to go to a restaurant and have a real seafood dinner. My mother argued with them, saying that she would cook a good meal, but my aunt won this round. We walked up to the corner of Georgia Avenue and Atlantic Avenues to a restaurant named Dock's Oyster House (still there today). This was the first time that I ever was in a real restaurant, not a bar, not the VFW, not the American Legion, and not the Naval Officers Club. As a little kid, I was amazed at this place because it did not smell like spilled beer and cigarettes. My mother ordered a small piece of fried flounder for me; I had never had flounder before, and I remember it tasted fantastic. The meal came with French fries—wow. This was the first time that I had a piece of fish that did not have bones in it. My mother would only buy the whole fish at home in Philly, and you had to pick out each and every little bone as you ate it—not enjoyable. We finished our meal and my aunt spoke quickly and said she wanted me to have dessert. I did not know how to react, as I never had a dessert after a meal at home.

My uncle took me to the beach the next day, and I do remember that we stayed longer than when my mother took me. My uncle even took me into the ocean, and I jumped over the waves as they rolled in. I had a fantastic day and still remember that time. My uncle took me on the boardwalk at night and spent a lot of money, as I think I went on every ride on the pier. My aunt and uncle left the next day to drive back to Virginia, and I will always remember the time that I spent with them in Atlantic City.

Clothes, Christmas, the Infamous Haircut, and Other Stuff

As I stated before, my mother hated to buy clothes for me, as I would only get one season out of them. Of course this did not include shoes. She would only buy the bare necessities for me, such as underwear, socks, one pair of dress pants, one or two shirts, and a winter coat that had to last for two winters. I did not have a dress coat for Sunday or special occasions. After the first winter season, my arms would grow and hang out of the bottom of the sleeves. My father (who picked up sewing on his own) would take the winter coat, take out the hem in the sleeves, and then line the exposed area with a FLANNEL material of a completely different color and style. The wear lines from where the original hem was showed up. I would wear this coat for the second winter season, and I did notice other kids looking at me. I was the only kid in school with this aborted winter coat. I had to wear this asshole winter coat to school and church.

My father would also take the hem out of my school trousers to possibly get another season out of them. I would get the same looks and stares when I went to school. We were not poor, but my mother had other priorities beside buying clothes for me. When I got to fourth grade, my aunt from Virginia would send a box full of her son's clothes for me to wear. The large box was addressed to "Master Richard Etherton." I was so excited to receive this box and anticipated what was inside it. The box contained trousers, shirts, and shorts or sweaters, depending on the season. The items were slightly worn but in good condition, and all were stylish, with no absurd colors or patterns. There wasn't a lot of clothing, but just enough to get me excited about having some decent clothes to wear to school. Some of the clothes would not fit me and my mother would throw them out. I called my aunt on the phone and thanked her over and over for the clothes. The box of clothes would arrive for both the fall and spring seasons until I reached eighth grade. I called this my "care package," which pissed off my mother.

My mother and I would go to town before school started to buy the bare necessities of clothing that I needed. This would include socks, underwear, one or two shirts, and, of course, new shoes. We always shopped at Lit Brothers Subway Store. Lit Brothers was an old tie department store in downtown Philly, which is no longer in business. The subway store was the basement of the store and located as you exited the subway. My mother always bought my clothes there, as they were on sale or last year's discontinued items. One year she decided to buy me dungarees, as jeans were called then. She was apparently tired of seeing my few pairs of so-called good trousers being ruined when I was playing. She bought two pairs along with some basic items and we rode the subway home. I was so excited to finally have a pair of dungarees just like the other boys in the neighborhood. I put them on and was confused as there was no fly or front zipper–the zipper was on the side of the pants. I said nothing to my mother, as I thought this was the latest style. I guessed that I would have to take them down when I had to pee.

I went around to my best friend's house to show off my new dungarees and go out and play. While I was there, his older sister came down the stairs and looked at me and said, "Richie has girl's jeans on." My friend and his brother and sister all started to laugh hysterically at me. I felt like a pile of shit and ran home. I rang our doorbell, as my mother always kept all of the doors locked so "no one could break in and rob us" (believe me, there was nothing in that house to steal). I asked my mother why I had girl's dungarees on, and that I was laughed at by my friends sister. She said, "Be quiet and wear them, there is nothing wrong with them, be happy that you have something to wear." I just looked at her in disbelief. This is my mother, who put me on the street in women's pants! I found my father in the basement and told him to look at these dungarees; there was no fly or zipper on the front–they were girl's pants. My father said, "You wear that your mother bought for you, she knows what is best." So here I was in girl's dungarees and being forced to wear them in public. Talk about being humiliated by your parents, this was disgusting. I made sure that I wore these shit pants out as fast as I could, sometimes even tearing holes in them myself. How you could humiliate your only child like this, I could never understand. On occasion, I would hear comments from my friend's sister when I went to his house. She would ask, "Where are your girl jeans?" I ask again why my mother forced me to wear girl's jeans.

* * *

Christmas in the fifties was a very special time for a child. My mother and father would purchase a real Christmas tree, usually from the local supermarket lot. The prices of these trees ranged from two dollars for a "basic Charlie Brown tree" and up to five dollars for a "rich guy tree." I didn't know any family on our street who had a fake aluminum tree. We would usually buy a three dollar tree the week before Christmas and drag it home to 15th Street. My father would put the tree in the backyard, and it would be brought in on Christmas Eve day. My father would actually nail a wooden tree stand (that was supplied with the tree), to the bottom of the tree trunk. There were the metal tree stands that held the tree trunk, and you filled the stand with water to keep the tree somewhat alive and keep the tree needles from falling off. We didn't buy one of these metal tree stands until I was about ten years old.

My father would hang the lights on the tree, along with an old metal foil star as the tree topper. This star looked as if it originated from WWI: bent, wrinkled, and looking like shit. The tree lights were the old type: when one bulb went out, they all went out. You had to remove each bulb and replace it with a new bulb until the string of lights would come on again.

Bringing in the tree, nailing on the tree stand, putting up the ugly star, and hanging the lights was the extent of my father's involvement in decorating the tree. My mother would bring out the Christmas balls, which were a collage of one box of fairly new balls and two boxes of things that matched the WWI tree star. She would proceed to hang these balls on the tree in a haphazard fashion. I was not allowed to touch any of the balls that were destined to go on the tree. "Don't touch the balls in the boxes, you will break them, these are very old." After all of the "precious balls" were hung on the tree, my mother would attempt to put the tinsel on the tree. Tinsel back then was actually thin strands of "lead." The tinsel was heavy and actually hung from each branch if placed on the tree branch correctly. My mother did not hang the tinsel strands but actually threw them on the tree. As I got older, I would have my small set of Lionel Trains running around the bottom of the tree. When a piece of the tinsel fell off the tree branch and landed on the train track, the tinsel would actually spark and short out the train track.

As a young boy, I thought our Christmas tree looked sick as compared to the trees at my friend's houses. Christmas Eve was like any other night at home. My mother would have the radio on during the day on Christmas Eve, and I would hear a few Christmas Carols. The radio would be turned off that night, and the normal ritual of Western cowboy TV shows would be playing. There were no Christmas carols on the radio, no hot chocolate or homemade cookies or treats left for Santa on Christmas Eve at 15th Street. I would wake up on Christmas morning and come downstairs to see what Santa had left for me. My toys were all in the bags from the stores where my parents had purchased them. Paper bags from Sears, Gimbels, Lit Brothers, Strawbridge and Clothier. NONE of my toys (supposedly from Santa), were in Christmas gift wrapping. There was never a Christmas gift-wrapped toy under the Christmas tree. We were not poor, as I have stated before; I received the usual number of toys at Christmas, BUT I never had a Christmas-wrapped present from my parents as long as I lived. When I asked my mother why my presents were not wrapped, she said, "I don't know how to wrap a present, don't question me, and be thankful for what you get, and stop complaining."

I remember that I would go around to my best friend's house on Christmas Day, (there were six children there), and I would see mounds of Christmas wrapping papers on the floor. The mother of these children found the time and effort to wrap each of her children's presents with love and caring in gala Christmas wrapping paper. I remember that scene to this day. I was probably in fourth grade when a friend of my mother's came over to visit her between Christmas and New Years. When this woman came through our front door, she handed me a package wrapped in Christmas paper. I thanked the lady and stared at the package in the beautiful Christmas wrapping paper. I didn't open the package for a while but just kept looking at it. My mother and the lady went into the kitchen and sat down and began talking. I finally opened the package, and it was a box of Play-Doh (molding clay for children). I took the Play-Doh into the kitchen and showed my mother, and thanked the lady for the gift. My mother immediately took the box away from me and said, "We will open this later," and then told me to go and play with my other Christmas toys. The lady left but I thanked her again for the gift. I asked my mother if I could open the Play-Doh now, but she said "NO, I will not have this clay all over the floors in this house; I will give this to one of the other children on the street." I felt hurt by her actions and could not understand why she had done this. Here was a woman, a complete stranger to me, not a relative, not a neighbor, thinking of me and spending the money for a gift, then taking the time to wrap the gift in Christmas paper. What was my mother's problem with wrapped Christmas gifts? The woman never visited our home again, but if she had, I wanted to tell her that my mother took her gift from me and gave it to someone else.

My aunt from South Philly would visit us on 15th Street every year between Christmas and New Years. She would always bring me a gift wrapped in beautiful Christmas paper. She would arrive around lunchtime and spend the afternoon with us. Her Christmas gift to me was always an article of clothing, a shirt, or a sweater. I really didn't care that she was giving me clothes, as I was grateful that someone thought enough about me to wrap up a Christmas present. Here we go again, my aunt taking the time to wrap a gift for me at Christmas. I could always count on receiving one wrapped gift at Christmas, but not from my mother.

***

I actually remember the day of the "infamous hair cut" fiasco; it was a Saturday afternoon in Spring, and we just came home from buying various dry goods at the Navy Commissary. After bringing the items into the house, my mother had her usual glass of the Christian Brothers Port Wine. It didn't take long for the goofy look on her face to emerge, which always happened when she drank. I was in sixth grade and starting to feel self-conscious about my appearance. I said that I wanted to get a haircut that afternoon. Mother gave me three dollars, which covered two dollars and fifty cents for the haircut and fifty cents for the tip to the barber (haircuts were reasonable in those days). We had a barbershop at the corner of 15th Street and Loudon Street, just a few steps from our house. I walked into the barbershop, and there were about four men waiting ahead of me. Finally, it was my turn in the chair, and I told the barber not to cut my hair too close, as I had noticed the other boy's haircuts in school did not look like mine. Clip, clip, away, and I was finished. I thanked the barber and gave the three dollars and I walked home. I saw my mother sitting on our porch, and as I grew closer, I noticed the telltale goofy look on her face from when she was drinking.

I came up the steps to our porch, and she had a ciggie half hanging out of her mouth. She looked at me and immediately said, "What type of a haircut is that? I gave you money to get a proper haircut, we are going back to the barbers now." She came down the steps, almost falling on her face. She walked (stumbled) with me back to the corner barbershop. We entered the barber shop, and now there were four to five men sitting there. The barber had a customer in the chair and asked, "Is there a problem?"

My mother immediately blurted out, "His hair is not cut the way that I want it cut, I want it cut properly ." The barber looked at her and said OK, wait your turn. I could see the men sitting around looking at me because I looked like an asshole because my mother had to bring me back to the barbershop to get my hair cut. I personally felt like a stupid idiot, being escorted back to the barbershop to get my hair cut the way SHE wanted it.

It seemed like an hour passed until it was my turn to sit in the chair again. The next act by my mother was an act of pure hatred and embarrassment to me. My mother came over to the barber chair and stood there and was telling the barber how she wanted my hair cut! There were about two more men who had entered the barber shop by now, and the looks and smirks on their faces told the whole story.

Here is a young man who is not allowed to have his hair cut the way that he wants it. I can only imagine the thoughts they had toward my mother, watching this shit show. My mother finally said to the barber, "This is a proper haircut now." I got out of the chair and left the barber shop as fast as I could, with my mother behind me hollering, "Richard, Richard, come back here now, I'm your mother." I completely ignored her and started walking as fast as I could, past our house, past Rockland Street, and up to Broad Street. I must have walked for an hour and finally went home. When I came into our house, Mother was sitting there, in the bag now, as she could hardly put a sentence together. I walked by her and went upstairs to my room and closed the door. At that moment I absolutely hated my mother for her actions on that day. I relieve this abomination every time I go to get my hair cut.

As I have previously stated, my wife Connie and my mother never got along, and my mother always held animosity toward Connie. I remember that it was about a month before we were to be married, my mother said to me, "This is not going to be a good marriage, if you want to get out of it, tell me, and I will talk to Connie's father." I looked at her, shook my head, and walked away. I didn't say anything, because if I did, I would have exploded on her.

I was always doing something around our house in Churchville, painting, electrical work, wallpapering, extensive gardening outside, etc. This was all done after I had finished spending my Saturday with my mother, which was every Saturday. My mother would always harp on me to stop doing all of this work on the house, sit down, rest, and stop all of the unnecessary work. My mother would talk to Connie's mom on the phone a few times a week. There was a specific phone call when my mother said to Connie's mom that "Connie should stop having Richard constantly working around the house, if something happens to him, who will want her at her age?" Such love from my mother!

Conclusions

My mother had no filter: she said and did whatever was on her mind, even if it brought tears to your eyes. A typical story was when my mother was visiting Virginia (with more than a few drinks under her belt) began to scream and holler at two of my cousins. She went into a disgusting tirate of calling their mother a low-life whore. For whatever reason, nobody will ever know. My mother was in her glory when she was arguing with you, for any reason. She could be in a fairly decent mood, and in the blink of an eye, she wanted to fight and argue with you, and for no apparent reason. Looking back now, I honestly believe that my mother was bipolar, as she could swing from one mood to another in a matter of moments.

When my mother first meets you, she would hit you with sixty questions: what nationality are you, how old are you, what parish are you from, did you go to church every Sunday, how stable is your job, did you serve during the war, and so on. She would then go into her standard, "I graduated from West Catholic Girls High School, I lived in South Philly, blah, blah, blah. My mother would blurt out remarks at people that you could not ignore or take back. Her comments would only grow in both intensity and disgust as she continued to drink. She was always looking to latch on to someone as a "drinking buddy," and she did find one or two, who did not last very long due to her changeable nature.

At my wedding reception, my best man whom I grew up with told my new wife Connie that "Everybody in the neighborhood would not be surprised if they heard that Richard went into the basement and hung himself because of his mother's bullshit."

You can have numerous fathers in your life, but everyone has only one mother. You should have both love and respect for your mother, but I can only muster a mediocre affection. As I look back through my experiences with the Gestapo penguins (nuns), I can now look at these turds as misfits incapable of having developing children in their charge. I honestly believe that the penguins were indoctrinated with hate for little boys, as they were in their training period at the Mother House. I understand completely that my mother's actions and words were defaming to both me and others that she met, all on an equal level. She never changed her methods or believed that she was doing wrong, or that her words were hurtful and cutting.

My mother passed away in 1996. I remember the priest's sermon at her requiem mass saying that "We all know that Irene will not be telling Jesus in heaven what to say or do."

Aside from all of the turmoil, and frustrations of growing up Catholic, I still have my faith and trust in God.